SLEEP

PARALYSIS

BY

E.A. Pier

Title: Sleep Paralysis
Author: E.A. Pier

This book is a work of nonfiction. While every effort has been made to ensure accuracy, the information contained herein is provided on an "as is" basis without warranty of any kind. The author and publisher disclaim all liability in connection with the use of this book.

ISBN:
First Edition

Published by E.A. Pier
Printed in United State

PREFACE

Sleep paralysis—an eerie and often terrifying phenomenon that straddles the line between wakefulness and sleep—has fascinated, frightened, and puzzled humanity for centuries. For those who experience it, the feeling of being awake yet unable to move, accompanied by vivid hallucinations and a sense of overwhelming fear, can be both profoundly disorienting and distressing. Despite its widespread occurrence, sleep paralysis has remained an enigma, largely misunderstood and relegated to the realm of superstition and myth in many cultures.

This book aims to unravel the mystery of sleep paralysis, shedding light on its scientific, psychological, and cultural dimensions while offering practical strategies for those affected by it. As someone who has worked closely with individuals experiencing this phenomenon, as well as having examined the rich history, science, and personal accounts of sleep paralysis, I have come to appreciate the multifaceted nature of this condition. It is not just a medical issue but also a profound psychological experience and, in some ways, a spiritual and cultural one.

Throughout these pages, we will explore the latest scientific research on the neurological and genetic causes of sleep paralysis. We will offer insights into why the brain sometimes wakes up before the body is ready and why certain individuals are more susceptible than others. We will dive into the psychological factors at play, from the role of anxiety and trauma to how our brains create vivid hallucinations when we are stuck between sleep and wakefulness.

Yet, this book is not merely a collection of clinical facts and data. The personal stories and case studies featured here offer a deeply human perspective, showing the impact that sleep paralysis has on individuals and how they cope with it. We will explore how different cultures interpret the experience, from the terrifying "old hag" or "night hag" in Western folklore to the Japanese concept of **kanashibari**, and the ways in which spiritual and supernatural beliefs have shaped people's understanding of sleep paralysis.

As we journey through these chapters, you will encounter a variety of practical strategies for coping with sleep paralysis—from techniques in mindfulness and relaxation to therapies like cognitive-behavioral therapy (CBT) and advancements in neurofeedback. These tools can help mitigate the fear, distress, and physical discomfort that many experience during episodes, empowering individuals to take control of their sleep health.

Moreover, this book doesn't just explore sleep paralysis as an isolated phenomenon. It places it within the broader context of consciousness studies and the fascinating world of lucid dreaming. For many, sleep paralysis is not just a condition to be feared but also an opportunity—a portal into the exploration of the mind's deepest layers. For some, the experience can even become a steppingstone to lucidity, where the ability to consciously control one's dreams offers newfound freedom and insight.

In the final chapters, we look ahead. What does the future hold for sleep paralysis research? How might advancements in neuroscience, genetic research, and sleep technology help us understand this condition more deeply and, perhaps, offer more effective treatments? The future of sleep paralysis research promises to be as fascinating and complex as the phenomenon itself, and it is with great hope that we anticipate solutions that may one day provide comfort and healing to those who suffer from it.

This book is written for anyone who has experienced sleep paralysis, for anyone curious about the phenomenon, and for those who seek to understand the intersection of science, culture, and human experience. It is for those who have struggled with the fear and anxiety that accompany sleep paralysis, as well as those who wish to explore the deeper mysteries of the human mind. I hope that by the time you finish these pages, you will feel empowered—whether you're seeking a way to reduce the frequency of episodes, searching for answers, or simply hoping to understand this strange and fascinating condition more fully.

TABLE OF CONTENT

CHAPTER OUTLINE AND OVERVIEW

Chapter 1: The First Encounter

- Introduce the phenomenon of sleep paralysis through vivid storytelling.
- Explore the emotional and physical experiences of individuals during their first encounters, drawing from real-life stories.
- Connect these personal narratives to broader patterns observed globally.

Chapter 2: What is Sleep Paralysis?

- Explain the scientific definition and physiological basis, such as the atonia in REM sleep.
- Delve into what distinguishes sleep paralysis from other sleep disorders.
- Share expert opinions and ongoing debates in neuroscience.

Chapter 3: Legends and Lore

- Examine historical and cultural interpretations of sleep paralysis, such as "The Old Hag" in Western cultures or supernatural encounters in Asian and African traditions.
- Analyze how folklore reflects human attempts to explain the unknown.

Chapter 4: New Age Perspectives on Sleep Paralysis: A Journey Beyond the Physical Realm

- **Gateway to Higher Awareness**: Sleep paralysis is seen as a unique opportunity to transcend physical reality and access heightened states of consciousness, connect with the higher self, or engage with metaphysical entities.
- **Astral Projection and Interdimensional Encounters**: The experience is often interpreted as a step in astral travel, where the soul may leave the body to explore other realms or as encounters with beings from other dimensions, influenced by the individual's energy and mindset.
- **Chakras and Energy Alignment**: Imbalances in energy centers, such as the third eye or crown chakra, are believed to contribute to sleep

paralysis, with practices like meditation, visualization, and energy healing recommended to prevent or navigate the experience.

Chapter 5: The Science of Sleep Paralysis

- Provide a foundational understanding of sleep stages, focusing on REM sleep and its connection to dreams.

- Introduce the neural and hormonal mechanisms behind sleep paralysis.

- Include case studies from sleep research labs.

Chapter 6: The Psychological Dimension of Sleep Paralysis

- Discuss why sleep paralysis often induces fear, including the role of the amygdala.

- Explore the psychological effects of hallucinations and the feeling of helplessness.

- Include testimonies from people who have overcome this fear.

Chapter 7: Common Triggers

- Highlight triggers like irregular sleep schedules, stress, substance use, and mental health conditions.

- Discuss real-life scenarios where these factors led to episodes.

- Offer insights from clinical studies on preventing triggers.

Chapter 8: Sleep Paralysis Through History

- **Cultural and Historical Interpretations:** Sleep paralysis has been attributed to supernatural encounters across eras, from ancient Egyptian beliefs in the soul's nocturnal journey to medieval fears of demon attacks and witchcraft trials, highlighting humanity's quest to explain the inexplicable.

- **Shifts Toward Scientific Inquiry:** The Renaissance and Enlightenment periods initiated a transition from spiritual explanations to medical theories, with figures like Paracelsus and Galen proposing early physiological insights, paving the way for modern sleep science.

- **Modern Understanding and Legacy:** Advances in neuroscience, including the discovery of REM sleep, redefined sleep paralysis as a neurological phenomenon. Despite this, cultural myths persist, reflecting the enduring interplay between science, belief, and human experience.

Chapter 9: The Neuroscience of Hallucinations

- Explain the link between sensory perception, dreams, and hallucinations during sleep paralysis.
- Share examples of common hallucinations, such as shadowy figures and pressure on the chest.
- Explore cutting-edge research in neurobiology.

Chapter 10: The Psychology of Sleep Paralysis

- Correlations between sleep paralysis and anxiety, depression, and PTSD.
- Highlight cases where therapy has helped individuals manage symptoms.
- Emphasize the importance of a holistic approach to mental health.

Chapter 11: Stories from the Shadows

- Compile a diverse collection of personal accounts from individuals around the world.

- Focus on both commonalities and unique cultural experiences.
- Include reflective commentary tying these stories to broader themes.

Chapter 12: Breaking Free

- Share strategies and coping mechanisms that have proven effective, such as mindfulness and cognitive behavioral techniques.
- Include scientific evidence supporting these solutions.
- Offer step-by-step guidance for readers.

Chapter 13: Sleep Paralysis as a Creative Force

- Explore how artists, writers, and musicians have transformed their experiences into creative inspiration.
- Provide examples from literature, film, and art.
- Discuss the psychological benefits of reframing sleep paralysis.

Chapter 14: Medical Interventions

- Discuss when and how to seek professional help for sleep paralysis.

- Include an overview of medications, sleep studies, and alternative therapies.
- Interview sleep specialists about their approach.

Chapter 15: The Future of Sleep Research

- Highlight advancements in sleep science, from brain imaging to AI-assisted research.
- Speculate on the future understanding and treatment of sleep paralysis.
- Connect these possibilities to the broader field of neuroscience.

Chapter 16: Embracing the Unknown

- Encourage readers to view sleep paralysis as an opportunity for self-discovery rather than a source of fear.
- Provide reflective exercises to deepen understanding of one's mind and body.
- End with a hopeful and empowering note.

Chapter 16: Integrating the Mystery—A Holistic Approach to Sleep Paralysis

- Integrating sleep paralysis requires blending scientific, psychological, and spiritual perspectives for deeper understanding.
- A balanced approach combines healthy sleep habits with mindfulness, therapy, and creative expression.
- Reframing sleep paralysis as an opportunity to transform fear into curiosity and fosters resilience.

Chapter 17: Bridging Science, Spirituality, and the Human Experience: The Mystery of Sleep Paralysis and the final chapter

- **The Interplay of Science and Spirit**: Sleep paralysis bridges the domains of biology and belief.
- **Creativity and Resilience**: The vivid and surreal nature of sleep paralysis inspires artistic expression, transforming fear into powerful works of art, literature, and music.
- **A Gateway to Discovery**: Sleep paralysis offers profound insights into the boundaries of consciousness, revealing the intricate balance of the brain's sleep-wake systems.

Chapter 1:
The First Encounter

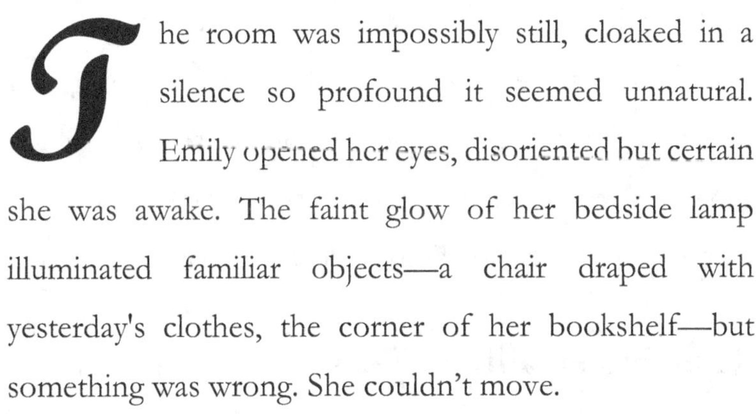

The room was impossibly still, cloaked in a silence so profound it seemed unnatural. Emily opened her eyes, disoriented but certain she was awake. The faint glow of her bedside lamp illuminated familiar objects—a chair draped with yesterday's clothes, the corner of her bookshelf—but something was wrong. She couldn't move.

Her chest felt as though an invisible weight pressed down, making each breath shallow and labored. She wanted to scream, to call for help, but her voice betrayed her, trapped as firmly as her limbs. Then she saw it. In the shadows near the doorway, a figure—featureless yet menacing—seemed to watch her. Emily's heart raced as cold dread seeped into her consciousness.

Moments later, the spell broke. Her body jerked as if released from invisible chains, and she gasped for air. The figure was gone. It had never been there. Yet the fear, visceral and raw, lingered long after the paralysis faded.

This is the story of countless others who have experienced the unnerving phenomenon known as sleep paralysis. It strikes without warning, often during the liminal spaces of sleep—just as the mind hovers between dreaming and waking. For some, it is a one-time ordeal, a strange glitch in their sleep cycle. For others, it becomes a recurring nightmare, each episode more terrifying than the last.

The Universality of Fear

Though Emily's story may sound like a scene from a horror movie, it is, in fact, a deeply human experience. Across cultures and continents, people have described eerily similar encounters. Some see shadowy figures; others feel unseen hands pinning them down. In almost every case, fear is the common thread.

"I thought I was dying," recalls Ahmed, a college student in Cairo who experienced sleep paralysis during a particularly stressful exam period. "I couldn't breathe, and there was this weight on my chest. I saw this...thing standing at the foot of my bed, staring at me. I still get chills thinking about it."

These first encounters with sleep paralysis often leave individuals grappling with questions. What just happened? Was it real? Am I losing my mind? The disorienting nature of the experience can blur the lines between dream and reality, plunging people into a state of confusion and fear.

The First Steps Toward Understanding

The fear and mystery surrounding sleep paralysis are compounded by its unpredictability. It can strike anyone, regardless of age, gender, or health. Historically, it was often attributed to supernatural forces. Medieval Europeans spoke of "the Old Hag," a malevolent entity that sat on victims' chests, suffocating them. In Japan, it is known as *kanashibari*, a term rooted in Buddhist traditions referring to being bound by spiritual forces.

Yet, as unsettling as these experiences are, modern science offers an alternative explanation. Sleep paralysis occurs when the body's natural mechanisms for entering and exiting REM sleep malfunction. During REM, the brain is highly active, and vivid dreams unfold, but the body remains paralyzed—a protective measure to prevent the physical enactment of dreams. Sleep paralysis happens when this paralysis persists even as the mind wakes up.

This physiological understanding, while comforting to some, doesn't erase the terror of the experience. For others, it raises even more questions: Why does it happen? Why does it feel so real?

A Shared, Silent Burden

Many who experience sleep paralysis suffer in silence, fearing judgment or disbelief if they share their stories. In a society that values rationality, discussing shadowy figures or sensations of suffocation can feel taboo.

"I didn't tell anyone for years," says Maria, a nurse from Mexico City. "I thought they'd think I was crazy or possessed. It wasn't until I read an article online that I realized it had a name—sleep paralysis—and I wasn't alone."

Maria's relief is echoed by countless others who discover they are not alone in their struggles. The moment of recognition—that this is a common, well-documented phenomenon—is often the first step toward demystifying and managing it.

Setting the Stage for Discovery

This book begins with the unsettling but deeply human experience of sleep paralysis because it is, at its core, a journey into the unknown. From the shadows of folklore to the bright lights of neuroscience labs, we will explore every facet of this phenomenon. Through personal stories, historical insights, and scientific evidence, we aim to provide a comprehensive understanding of what sleep paralysis is—and what it is not.

But more than understanding, this book is about reclaiming power. For too long, sleep paralysis has been a source of fear, a mystery that leaves its victims feeling helpless. By unraveling its secrets, we can transform this experience into one of curiosity, resilience, and, ultimately, mastery.

For those who have felt the icy grip of paralysis, this journey is for you. And for those who have never experienced it, prepare to enter a world where the boundaries between dream and reality blur—a world as fascinating as it is unsettling.

Let us begin.

Chapter 2:

What is Sleep Paralysis?

Sleep paralysis is a strange crossroads between the conscious and unconscious mind, where the ordinary rules of reality seem to falter. For those who experience it, the sensation is visceral: eyes open, thoughts racing, yet the body remains stubbornly unresponsive. But what exactly is sleep paralysis? Is it a glitch in our biology or a gateway to some deeper, unexplored realm of consciousness?

To understand this enigmatic condition, we must first strip away its layers, exploring both its biological foundation and the lived experiences of those who endure it.

The Science Behind the Stillness

At its core, sleep paralysis is a sleep disorder categorized within the broader family of parasomnia, which also includes phenomena like sleepwalking and night terrors. It occurs during the transition between wakefulness and rapid eye movement (REM) sleep, either as the person is falling asleep (*hypnagogic sleep paralysis*) or waking up (*hypnopompic sleep paralysis*).

In REM sleep, the body undergoes a natural process called *atonia*, where the brain sends signals to temporarily paralyze the voluntary muscles. This paralysis is a safeguard, preventing us from physically acting out our dreams. Normally, atonia ceases when we transition out of REM sleep and awaken. But in sleep paralysis, this system malfunctions. The mind becomes conscious while the body remains immobilized, creating a stark and terrifying dissonance.

Neurologist Dr. Rachel Liang explains, "Imagine waking up to find yourself locked in your own body. You're aware of your surroundings, but your brain's motor cortex hasn't reactivated yet. It's a physiological mismatch, like trying to drive a car when the ignition won't turn."

This physiological phenomenon might sound straightforward, but for those who experience it, the reality feels anything but.

Hallucinations or Something More?

Complicating the experience of sleep paralysis are the vivid hallucinations that often accompany it. These sensory phenomena can range from the benign—a feeling of floating or hearing faint whispers—to the profoundly disturbing, such as shadowy figures looming in the room or sensations of being suffocated.

Research suggests these hallucinations arise from the brain's attempt to reconcile conflicting signals. During REM sleep, the brain's visual and auditory centers are active, generating dream imagery and sounds. When consciousness returns prematurely during sleep paralysis, these dream elements can spill over into waking perception, blurring the boundaries between reality and imagination.

Interestingly, hallucinations during sleep paralysis tend to follow predictable patterns across cultures and individuals. These fall into three main categories:

1 **The Intruder**: A perceived presence in the room, often malevolent or threatening.

2 **The Incubus**: A feeling of pressure on the chest, accompanied by difficulty breathing, as if something is sitting or lying on the victim.

3 **Vestibular-Motor Hallucinations**: Sensations of floating, flying, or being pulled out of the body, sometimes interpreted as out-of-body experiences.

These shared patterns suggest that sleep paralysis taps into deep, primal parts of the brain—regions responsible for fear and survival instincts. "The Intruder archetype, for example, might be an exaggerated response of the brain's hypervigilance network," says Dr. Liang. "It's as though the brain, sensing vulnerability during paralysis, creates a predator to justify its fear."

How Common Is It?

Sleep paralysis is far from rare. Studies indicate that approximately 8-10% of the global population will experience it at least once in their lifetime, though rates vary by demographic and geography. It is more prevalent among adolescents and young adults, with episodes often triggered by irregular sleep patterns, stress, and sleep deprivation.

For some, sleep paralysis is a rare and fleeting curiosity. For others, it becomes chronic, recurring multiple times a month or even weekly. This chronic form can have significant psychological impacts, including heightened anxiety, disrupted sleep, and, in severe cases, depression.

Voices from the Void

Understanding sleep paralysis is not just about examining neurons and neurotransmitters; it's about listening to those who live through it.

James, a 29-year-old graphic designer from New York, recalls his first episode: "I was lying on my back, and suddenly I couldn't move. I felt this immense weight on my chest like someone was sitting on me. Then I saw a figure—black, faceless—standing in the corner of my room. It was watching me. I don't know how long it lasted, but it felt like hours. When it was over, I couldn't sleep for days."

Such accounts are chillingly common. The vividness of these episodes often leaves an indelible mark, making it difficult for people to dismiss them as mere "sleep glitches."

Bridging the Gap Between Science and Experience

What makes sleep paralysis so fascinating—and so difficult to comprehend—is the way it straddles the line between biology and personal perception. On one hand, it is a well-documented phenomenon with clear physiological underpinnings. On the other hand, it plunges individuals into deeply subjective, often surreal experiences that defy easy explanations.

Some researchers argue that sleep paralysis offers a rare glimpse into the workings of the unconscious mind. "It's as though the brain is briefly caught between two worlds," says psychologist Dr. Elena Morales. "The rational, waking mind and the dreamlike, symbolic realm of the subconscious collide, creating an experience that feels otherworldly."

Toward a Fuller Understanding

By the end of this chapter, the framework for understanding sleep paralysis begins to take shape. It is a physiological event, yes, but one that is inextricably tied to our psychology, culture, and even spirituality. The paralysis, the hallucinations, the fear—they are all pieces of a larger puzzle.

In the chapters to come, we will delve deeper into each of these elements. What do historical accounts of sleep paralysis reveal about humanity's evolving understanding of it? What role do cultural beliefs play in shaping how people interpret their experiences? And perhaps most importantly, how can we break free from its grip?

For now, we leave the realm of definitions and theories, stepping into the shadowy spaces where science meets the unknown. The journey is only just beginning.

This chapter expands the foundational understanding of sleep paralysis by blending scientific explanations with real-life experiences and psychological insights. It sets the stage for the exploration of cultural, historical, and practical aspects in subsequent chapters.

Chapter 3:

Legends and Lore

Long before the term "sleep paralysis" entered the lexicon of science, humanity sought to explain the strange and terrifying phenomenon that left individuals trapped in their bodies, paralyzed and vulnerable. These explanations often wove themselves into the fabric of myth, folklore, and religious belief, painting a vivid tapestry of cultural interpretations. From malevolent spirits to divine punishments, these stories reveal not just the fear of sleep paralysis but also the creativity and resilience of the human mind in its attempts to understand the unknown.

This chapter delves into the legends and lore surrounding sleep paralysis, exploring how different cultures have interpreted these episodes through the ages. These stories, while varied, often share strikingly similar themes, suggesting a universal human struggle to reconcile the boundaries of consciousness.

The "Old Hag" of European Folklore

In medieval Europe, sleep paralysis was often attributed to a witch or malevolent spirit, colloquially known as the "Old Hag." This spectral figure was said to sit on the chests of her victims, suffocating them and preventing their escape. The term "hagridden" emerged to describe the afflicted, linking their experiences to the supernatural.

These tales served as more than mere explanations; they were cautionary stories. The "Old Hag" often targeted individuals who had committed social or moral transgressions, reinforcing communal norms. If you stayed out late, neglected your prayers, or harbored grudges, you might wake up to her crushing weight on your chest—a grim reminder of your misdeeds.

Many firsthand accounts from the time mirror modern descriptions of sleep paralysis, with individuals reporting an overwhelming sense of dread, a heavy pressure on their bodies, and the presence of a dark, shadowy figure. The universality of these experiences lends credence to the theory that real physiological phenomena inspired such legends.

Kanashibari: Japan's Spiritual Binding

In Japan, sleep paralysis is known as *kanashibari*. Kanashibari is often attributed to supernatural causes, particularly malevolent spirits, ghosts, or otherworldly entities. These forces are believed to restrain the body, leaving the individual awake but incapable of moving. This interpretation stems from Japan's long-standing belief in *yūrei*—restless spirits who linger in the mortal world due to unfinished business, strong emotions, or unresolved grudges. The paralysis associated with kanashibari is thought to occur when one of these spirits exerts its presence, seeking to communicate or enact revenge.

Many stories in Japanese folklore reinforce this connection, often linking *kanashibari* to the presence of vengeful spirits or ghosts, known as *yūrei*. These entities are believed to bind their victims as a form of retribution, holding them captive between the realms of life and death. Stories of *kanashibari* frequently describe the victim sensing a figure hovering nearby, sometimes whispering or pressing down on their chest.

The vivid hallucinations that accompany kanashibari are explained as direct interactions with these spirits, whose presence is so overwhelming that it affects the physical world. The sensation of being watched or the oppressive weight on one's body during sleep paralysis aligns perfectly with these cultural narratives, further cementing the spiritual interpretation.

Kanashibari is not only confined to ghostly encounters; it is also linked to practices of spiritual binding in esoteric traditions. In some cases, kanashibari was intentionally induced as part of occult rituals. Practitioners believed they could immobilize an enemy or control a person's movements through spiritual means, invoking deities or forces to "bind" the individual. This practice, while rare and often associated with ancient rituals, illustrates how the concept of kanashibari extends beyond personal experience into a broader societal and mystical context.

The psychological and emotional landscape of Japan also plays a role in shaping the experience of kanashibari. Japanese culture emphasizes harmony and collective well-being and suppressed emotions or unresolved stress are often internalized rather than openly expressed. It is believed that

These pent-up emotions can manifest during sleep paralysis, with kanashibari serving as both a symptom of inner turmoil and a message from the spiritual realm urging resolution. For example, guilt, regret, or fear might be interpreted as attracting malevolent spirits or intensifying the spiritual connection to the experience.

In addition to its spiritual connotations, kanashibari has appeared in Japanese literature, art, and popular media. Classic works of literature often depict kanashibari as a terrifying yet almost inevitable phenomenon, a reflection of the tenuous boundary between the physical and spiritual worlds. Similarly, modern horror films and anime frequently draw on the concept to evoke fear, portraying characters immobilized by unseen forces. This portrayal perpetuates the cultural association of sleep paralysis with supernatural elements, keeping the idea of kanashibari alive in contemporary Japanese consciousness.

While Japan has embraced scientific advancements, the dual lens of spirituality and science is often applied to phenomena like kanashibari. On the one hand, sleep paralysis is understood medically as the result of disrupted REM sleep and temporary atonia. On the other hand, many still interpret the experience through a spiritual framework, especially in cases where hallucinations involve traditionally feared entities or occur in culturally significant contexts, such as during periods of mourning or in haunted locations.

Coping mechanisms for kanashibari in Japan often involve both practical and spiritual approaches. On a spiritual level, individuals might perform purification rituals, visit shrines, or seek the assistance of a priest or monk to ward off malevolent spirits. Protective charms, known as *omamori*, are also popular and are carried or placed near the bed to ensure a peaceful night's sleep. These practices not only offer a sense of security but also connect individuals to their cultural heritage, providing comfort in the face of unexplained phenomena.

From a modern perspective, the enduring belief in kanashibari reflects Japan's ability to blend ancient traditions with contemporary understanding. Sleep paralysis, while explained scientifically, continues to be viewed as a bridge between the natural and supernatural, a moment when the veil between worlds grows thin. For those who experience it, kanashibari remains both a terrifying ordeal and a profound reminder of the unseen forces that, for many in Japan, still shape their world.

a term that translates roughly to "bound by metal." This concept has its roots in Buddhist teachings, where the word originally referred to the ability of monks to immobilize others through spiritual power. Over time, it evolved into a term describing the paralysis felt during sleep.

Even in modern Japan, *kanashibari* retains its mystical connotations. Surveys indicate that a significant portion of the population has experienced it, and many still interpret it through the lens of traditional beliefs despite scientific explanations.

The Djinn of the Middle East

In Islamic tradition, sleep paralysis is often attributed to the djinn, supernatural beings mentioned in the Qur'an. These entities, made of smokeless fire, are said to inhabit a parallel world that exists alongside the human realm. Djinns are complex beings endowed with free will, capable of both good and evil. While some djinns are benevolent or neutral, others are believed to harbor malice, their actions driven by jealousy, revenge, or pure mischief. This duality makes them a source of both fascination and fear, particularly when it comes to their connection with sleep paralysis.

Accounts of djinn-induced sleep paralysis often describe an overwhelming sense of dread. Those afflicted report feeling a sinister presence in the room, one that seems to lurk just out of sight. This presence is frequently accompanied by an oppressive weight on the chest, making it difficult to breathe, as though an unseen force is pinning the person down. Hallucinations during these episodes can include hearing whispers in an unknown language, sometimes guttural and menacing, as well as sensations of being touched or restrained by invisible hands. These vivid and terrifying experiences align closely with the traditional narratives surrounding djinn, further strengthening their association with sleep paralysis in Islamic and Middle Eastern cultures.

For many believers, the djinn offers a framework to understand what an inexplicable and isolating event might otherwise be. The Qur'an explicitly acknowledges the existence of djinn and their interactions with humans, adding a spiritual dimension to episodes of sleep paralysis. This perspective transforms the experience from a purely physical or psychological phenomenon into one of spiritual significance. Many individuals turn to their faith for protection during such moments, reciting verses from the Qur'an to dispel the djinn and break the paralysis. Ayat al-Kursi (The Throne Verse) and Surah Al-Falaq are particularly favored for their perceived power to ward off malevolent entities. The act of recitation often brings comfort and relief, reinforcing the belief that divine intervention can counter the djinn's influence.

The interplay between cultural beliefs and individual perception is especially evident in these accounts. The djinn's role in sleep paralysis is deeply embedded in the collective consciousness of Islamic and Middle Eastern societies, shaping how people interpret and respond to their experiences. For some, the belief in djinn explains the vivid and terrifying hallucinations that accompany sleep paralysis, offering a narrative that aligns with their spiritual worldview. This interpretation also emphasizes the vulnerability of the human soul during sleep, a state seen as a liminal space where the boundaries between the physical and spiritual worlds blur.

Culturally, the djinn is often associated with liminal spaces and moments of transition. They are believed to inhabit deserted places, ruins, and the shadows of night, making sleep an opportune time for encounters. In Middle Eastern folklore, tales of djinn-induced paralysis are common, passed down through generations as cautionary stories. These narratives often include moral lessons or warnings about respecting the unseen world. For example, disturbing a djinn's dwelling—whether knowingly or unknowingly—is thought to provoke their wrath, resulting in experiences such as sleep paralysis. Such stories reinforce cultural norms about coexistence with the unseen and the need for spiritual vigilance.

In modern times, the scientific understanding of sleep paralysis as a disruption in the REM cycle and the temporary paralysis that accompanies it offers an alternative explanation. However, for many, this physiological perspective coexists with traditional beliefs. The djinn remains a potent symbol of the unseen and inexplicable, embodying the fear and awe that arise from encounters with forces beyond human comprehension. Even in urban and educated societies, the stories of djinn-induced sleep paralysis endure, reflecting the deep cultural and spiritual roots of these beliefs.

The enduring power of the djinn in the narrative of sleep paralysis highlights humanity's need to make sense of the unknown. By framing these episodes through the lens of the djinn, individuals not only find an explanation but also a connection to a broader cultural and spiritual tradition. Whether viewed as a test of faith, a warning from the unseen, or a manifestation of spiritual vulnerability, the djinn remains an integral part of how sleep paralysis is understood in the Middle East, blending fear, reverence, and the timeless allure of the supernatural.

Indigenous Interpretations

Among Indigenous cultures in North America, sleep paralysis often transcends the physical realm, taking on profound spiritual or shamanic significance. For the Inuit of Canada, this mysterious phenomenon is deeply entwined with their worldview, in which the boundaries between the natural and supernatural are fluid. The experience of sleep paralysis is frequently attributed to *ujirat*, a shapeshifting spirit that is both feared and respected. According to Inuit belief, *ujirat* does not merely haunt the physical body; it delivers a powerful message from the spirit world. When someone is paralyzed and gripped by vivid hallucinations, it is often interpreted as a punishment or test, triggered by their failure to adhere to taboos or heed the wisdom of their elders.

For the Inuit, taboos are not just social constructs but sacred guidelines that maintain harmony with the spiritual and natural worlds. Breaking these taboos—be it through disrespecting nature, failing to honor ancestral traditions, or acting selfishly—disrupts this balance. The arrival of *ujirat* during sleep paralysis is, therefore, seen as a direct consequence of such transgressions, forcing the individual to confront their misdeeds in an intensely personal and often terrifying manner. The paralysis itself is a symbolic restraint, a moment of enforced stillness that compels the person to reflect on their actions.

Similarly, in many African cultures, sleep paralysis carries heavy spiritual implications, often tied to witchcraft or supernatural attacks. Here, experience is rarely viewed as a mere quirk of biology but rather as evidence of unseen forces at work. Victims commonly believe that envious neighbors, estranged relatives, or those harboring ill will have summoned malevolent spirits to harm them. The hallucinatory aspects of sleep paralysis—shadowy figures, whispered incantations, or a suffocating presence—are interpreted as manifestations of these dark intentions. Such episodes are viewed as direct assaults on the soul, where the victim's vulnerability during sleep makes them an easy target for spiritual manipulation.

Among some African communities, this interpretation of sleep paralysis also ties into the broader societal dynamics of trust and conflict. Accusations of witchcraft are often directed at those who are perceived as outsiders or as having unresolved grievances with the victim. Sleep paralysis thus becomes a highly charged event, not just for the individual experiencing it but for the community as a whole. Rituals of protection or cleansing are frequently employed to counteract these perceived spiritual attacks, ranging from prayer and herbal remedies to elaborate ceremonies involving a spiritual leader or shaman.

Across these diverse cultures, a striking commonality emerges: sleep paralysis is rarely seen as a random or meaningless occurrence. Whether attributed to *ujirat*, malevolent spirits, or witchcraft, the phenomenon is imbued with deep significance. It serves as a moral lesson, a spiritual test, or a warning from the unseen world. These interpretations offer both an explanation for the experience and a way to restore balance, whether through introspection, reconciliation, or communal intervention.

This cultural framing transforms sleep paralysis into something far more than a transient physiological state. It becomes a narrative, a moment of reckoning where the spiritual and moral dimensions of life are laid bare. For those within these traditions, the experience is not just terrifying but profoundly meaningful. It is a reminder of the unseen forces that shape their world and the responsibilities they bear to honor them. This perspective, rooted in ancient wisdom and spiritual intuition, offers a fascinating lens through which to understand the intersection of culture, belief, and the mysterious workings of the human mind.

Shared Themes Across Cultures

Despite the immense variety of cultural interpretations, certain recurring motifs weave through the rich tapestry of sleep paralysis lore. Across continents and traditions, the experience seems to evoke a shared narrative of terror and vulnerability, with elements that resonate deeply with primal human fears. One of the most pervasive themes is the presence of a malevolent entity, often described in stark and terrifying detail. Whether it takes the form of a witch perched on the chest, a shadowy ghost looming in the corner, or the sinister figure of a djinn whispering in an unknown language, this hostile presence is a central figure in the sleep paralysis experience. The universal nature of this imagery suggests a fundamental human fear of being attacked by something beyond comprehension. This predator strikes not in the waking world but in the liminal space between sleep and consciousness.

The physical sensation of chest pressure, often described as suffocating or crushing, adds another layer of horror. Across cultures, this feeling is frequently attributed to the weight of the malevolent entity itself. In European traditions, the entity may be depicted as a hag or a witch, pressing down to steal the breath of the victim. In other regions, it might be a demon, a ghost, or even a shapeshifting spirit exacting punishment. The inability to breathe freely not only evokes an acute sense of physical vulnerability but also heightens the psychological distress of the moment. This sensation of being trapped and unable to escape mirrors ancient fears of helplessness, predation, and powerlessness in the face of danger.

Equally compelling is the way sleep paralysis is often interpreted as a moral or spiritual reckoning. In many cultural narratives, the episode is not a random occurrence but a direct consequence of the sufferer's actions—or lack thereof. A person might be paralyzed because they have violated sacred taboos, neglected spiritual practices, or committed moral transgressions. The entity becomes a harbinger of justice, delivering a punishment that forces the individual to confront their failings. In this way, sleep paralysis serves as both a terror-inducing event and a moment of profound reflection, where the boundaries between the spiritual, moral, and psychological realms blur.

These recurring themes—an oppressive presence, the sensation of chest pressure, and the attribution of moral or spiritual causation—reveal a shared thread running through humanity's collective psyche. The inability to move, combined with the sense of being watched or attacked, activates ancient survival instincts buried deep within the brain. These instincts, honed over millennia of evolution, are designed to respond to threats with fight-or-flight reactions.

Yet, in the paralyzed state of sleep, these instincts become trapped, transforming into fertile ground for fear to take root.

What makes these experiences even more compelling is the way they are filtered through cultural and individual lenses. While the underlying sensations and psychological triggers may be universal, their interpretation is deeply influenced by personal beliefs and cultural narratives. A villager in a remote corner of the world might see the shadowy figure as a witch exacting revenge for a perceived slight, while someone steeped in Islamic tradition might recognize the presence of a djinn testing their faith. These interpretations lend a sense of structure and meaning to an otherwise bewildering event, reinforcing the idea that sleep paralysis is not merely a biological anomaly but a moment fraught with symbolic and emotional significance.

This interplay between universal sensations and culturally specific interpretations highlights how sleep paralysis bridges the realms of science, psychology, and folklore. The phenomenon taps into something deeply embedded in the human experience—a primal fear of being hunted, controlled, or overpowered by forces beyond our understanding. At the same time, it reflects humanity's need to assign meaning to the inexplicable, transforming a moment of terror into a narrative of accountability, survival, or spiritual connection. The shared motifs found in sleep paralysis lore are not just echoes of ancient fears but also profound reminders of how interconnected we are in our responses to the mysteries of the mind and the night.

From Superstition to Science

While modern science offers physiological explanations for sleep paralysis, the persistence of folklore highlights the power of storytelling in shaping human understanding. For centuries, these legends provided comfort and meaning, transforming a terrifying and incomprehensible experience into something that could be named, discussed, and even battled.

Interestingly, even as science advances, many people continue to blend traditional beliefs with modern insights. For instance, someone might acknowledge the biological mechanisms of sleep paralysis while still attributing their hallucinations to a spiritual encounter. This duality reflects the complex interplay between culture, biology, and personal perception.

Why Folklore Still Matters

The Stories about sleep paralysis are more than reflections of our fears—they are evidence of our enduring need to understand and make sense of the unexplainable. These narratives, born from encounters with shadowy figures, suffocating weight, and unseen forces, reveal the depth of human imagination and our determination to weave order out of chaos. Across cultures and generations, the legends of sleep paralysis transform moments of terror into meaningful stories, offering explanations that resonate with the beliefs, fears, and hopes of those who tell them.

They reveal a universal truth: in the face of the mysterious and the unknown, we are driven not to retreat but to create.

These stories, filled with witches, spirits, djinn, and phantoms, transcend their time and place, connecting us to a shared human experience. They are not merely relics of superstition; they are acts of resilience, attempts to understand and even tame the overwhelming. They take what feels incomprehensible—the paralysis, the hallucinations, the oppressive dread—and ground it in a narrative that speaks to something greater, whether spiritual, moral, or psychological. In doing so, they bridge the gap between personal experience and collective understanding, transforming isolation into connection.

By examining these myths and beliefs, we gain a profound appreciation for their cultural depth and their ability to illuminate the human psyche. They reflect a deep-seated need to find structure in the shapeless, to frame moments of vulnerability within a larger narrative that gives them purpose. These tales are not just reactions to fear but expressions of hope—the hope that understanding, even in its most imaginative form, can provide comfort, perspective, and a sense of control over the uncontrollable.

Let us pause here, in this realm of shadows, where the boundaries between fear and creativity blur. Here, in the stories of spirits and specters, we see humanity's ability to shine light into the darkest recesses of the unknown. These legends remind us of the power of storytelling, not just to recount events but to shape our understanding of them, transforming fleeting moments of terror into enduring narratives of meaning and resilience. As we prepare to delve into the mechanics of sleep itself, these stories linger, whispering of the timeless interplay between the mysteries of the mind and the boundless creativity of the human spirit.

Chapter 4:

New Age Perspectives on Sleep Paralysis, A Journey Beyond the Physical Realm

In New Age perspectives, sleep paralysis is often viewed through a lens that blends spirituality, metaphysics, and holistic understanding. While modern science explains sleep paralysis as a disruption in the REM sleep cycle, New Age interpretations often frame it as an experience that transcends the physical realm, offering unique insights into consciousness and the spiritual journey.

One common belief in New Age circles is that sleep paralysis represents a gateway to higher states of awareness. Many practitioners see the state as a moment of heightened sensitivity, where the boundaries between the physical and spiritual worlds blur. In this view, paralysis and accompanying hallucinations are not malfunctions of the brain but rather opportunities for spiritual growth and exploration. Individuals experiencing sleep paralysis might be encouraged to see it as a chance to connect with their higher self, spirit guides, or other metaphysical entities.

Astral projection is another concept frequently linked to sleep paralysis in New Age thought. Some believe that the sensation of being immobilized, along with feelings of detachment from the body, indicates that the soul is in the process of leaving or returning to the physical form. During sleep paralysis, individuals may feel as though they are floating or hovering outside their bodies—a phenomenon interpreted by New Age adherents as the beginning of an astral journey. Proponents often suggest embracing the experience and attempting to move the consciousness beyond the physical body to explore higher dimensions.

The presence of shadowy figures or entities, often described during sleep paralysis episodes, is sometimes understood within New Age philosophy as encounters with interdimensional beings. These beings may be seen as neutral, benevolent, or even malevolent, depending on the individual's mindset and energy vibrations. New Age perspectives often emphasize the importance of maintaining a positive and fearless attitude during such episodes, as fear is thought to attract lower-vibrational entities. Practices like energy shielding, visualization, and calling upon protective spirits or deities are recommended to navigate these encounters safely.

New Age teachings also explore the role of chakras and energy flow in sleep paralysis. Disruptions in the body's energy centers, particularly the third eye or crown chakra, are believed to contribute to the phenomenon. Meditation, energy healing, and aligning the chakras are suggested as preventative and therapeutic measures. By balancing one's energy and cultivating inner harmony, practitioners believe they can reduce the frequency and intensity of sleep paralysis episodes.

From a broader perspective, sleep paralysis is often seen as a reflection of one's spiritual and emotional state. Stress, unresolved fears, and suppressed emotions are thought to lower one's vibration, making sleep paralysis more likely and potentially more distressing. Conversely, a peaceful and balanced life is believed to reduce vulnerability to such experiences. For this reason, New Age practices often emphasize mindfulness, holistic health, and spiritual cleansing as tools to create a protective and harmonious energy field.

Ultimately, the New Age interpretation of sleep paralysis offers a perspective that transforms what is typically considered a distressing and involuntary condition into an opportunity for self-discovery and spiritual enlightenment. By framing sleep paralysis as a moment of spiritual potential, this viewpoint encourages individuals to face their fears, explore their consciousness, and deepen their connection to the universe.

Chapter 5:
The Science of Sleep Paralysis

To understand sleep paralysis fully, we must first venture into the intricate workings of sleep itself—a state far more dynamic and complex than it appears. Sleep is not merely a time when the body and mind shut down. It is an active, highly structured process involving distinct stages and cycles, each serving essential purposes for physical health and mental well-being. Within this delicate architecture lies the mystery of sleep paralysis, a phenomenon that emerges from disruptions in the finely balanced mechanisms of the brain during sleep.

Sleep unfolds in cycles, each lasting roughly 90 to 120 minutes, and these cycles repeat several times during the night. They are marked by shifts between two main categories: Non-Rapid Eye Movement (NREM) sleep and Rapid Eye Movement (REM) sleep. These stages are not random but are tightly coordinated, ensuring that the body and mind undergo vital restorative processes. Each stage is a building block, contributing to the holistic function of sleep, from repairing tissues and bolstering immunity to consolidating memories and regulating emotions.

NREM sleep begins the night's journey into slumber. It progresses through increasingly deeper stages, starting with the light drift of Stage N1, where the boundary between wakefulness and sleep is most fragile. Here, the mind begins to disengage, and the body starts to relax, though sudden muscle twitches, known as hypnic jerks, can momentarily break the serenity. Stage N2 is where true sleep sets in, marked by a slowdown in heart rate, a drop in body temperature, and the brain's heightened ability to filter out external distractions.

The final phase of NREM, Stage N3—or deep sleep—is a time of profound physical recovery. Growth hormones are released, tissues are repaired, and the immune system is fortified. During this stage, the brain exhibits low activity, allowing the body to focus on rejuvenation.

After NREM sleep, the body transitions into the enigmatic realm of REM sleep. Here, the brain becomes highly active, nearly mirroring wakefulness, while the body is placed in a state of profound stillness called atonia—a complete paralysis of voluntary muscles. This state is a safeguard, ensuring that even the most vivid and intense dreams remain confined to the mind and are not acted out physically. REM sleep is where imagination reigns supreme, dreams are born, and the brain processes emotions, consolidates memories, and engages in complex problem-solving. It is in this delicate and dream-filled stage that sleep paralysis finds its roots.

Atonia, the body's temporary paralysis during REM sleep, is central to the experience of sleep paralysis. During normal REM sleep, the brainstem sends signals to the spinal cord to inhibit motor activity, effectively immobilizing the body while the brain conjures its dreamscapes. This protective mechanism ensures that the dreamer remains safely at rest, no matter how active the mind might be. However, in the case of sleep paralysis, this intricate system falters. The sleeper's consciousness awakens prematurely, while atonia persists, trapping the individual in a twilight state of awareness but with no ability to move.

This jarring disconnect between mind and body creates the hallmark sensations of sleep paralysis: the eerie awareness of being awake, the inability to speak or move, and, for many, the disquieting feeling of an unseen presence. It is as if the mind is caught between worlds, straddling the boundary between the waking state and REM's dream-filled depths.

The reasons why atonia persists beyond its intended phase can often be traced back to disruptions in the sleep cycle. Irregular sleep schedules, such as those caused by jet lag or shift work, can fragment the smooth transitions between sleep stages, increasing the likelihood of sleep paralysis. Sleep deprivation adds to the risk, as a lack of restorative rest puts additional strain on the body's ability to regulate these transitions.

Stress and anxiety, too, play a significant role, altering brain chemistry in ways that make the boundaries between sleep and wakefulness more porous. In some cases, underlying sleep disorders such as narcolepsy or sleep apnea amplify the likelihood of these episodes, creating a recurring cycle of disrupted sleep and heightened vulnerability.

Understanding these processes helps illuminate how sleep paralysis occurs, but it also underscores the delicate balance that defines sleep itself. Each stage and cycle is a testament to the brain's complexity, a nightly symphony of activity and restoration. When this harmony is disrupted, the result is not merely fatigue or disorientation—it can manifest as an experience that feels profoundly otherworldly, like sleep paralysis, where the realms of dreams and reality collide

The Neurobiology of Sleep

To further understand sleep paralysis, we must examine the brain's role in sleep. Several key regions and neurotransmitters are involved in regulating sleep and wakefulness:

The Brainstem

The brainstem plays a crucial role in regulating the delicate balance between sleep and wakefulness, serving as the body's central "switch" for transitioning between these states. Deeply embedded in the brain's architecture, this structure ensures the synchronization of neural and physiological processes that maintain healthy sleep cycles. During rapid eye movement (REM) sleep, a stage associated with vivid dreaming, the brainstem takes on the vital task of sending inhibitory signals to the spinal cord. These signals effectively "turn off" voluntary muscle movement, a process known as atonia, preventing the body from physically acting out dreams.

In cases of sleep paralysis, this carefully orchestrated system experiences a timing mismatch. The brainstem's inhibition mechanism may remain active even as other areas of the brain responsible for consciousness begin to wake. This results in a disconcerting phenomenon where the individual is fully aware of their surroundings but unable to move their body. The feeling of paralysis can be particularly unsettling, as it directly contradicts the waking mind's expectation of motor control.

The timing of these processes is controlled by complex interactions between various neurotransmitters in the brainstem. For instance, during REM sleep, excitatory signals promoting vivid dreams coexist with inhibitory pathways that suppress physical activity. A disruption in this intricate balance can lead to the persistence of atonia after waking, creating the paralyzing sensation characteristic of sleep paralysis. The brainstem, in essence, becomes a crossroads where conflicting signals from different neural regions overlap, leading to this unique and often mysterious experience.

Sleep paralysis episodes tied to brainstem activity often come with heightened sensory perceptions, such as vivid hallucinations or an amplified sense of fear. These sensations are linked to the brainstem's interaction with the amygdala, the brain's emotional center, which tends to become hyperactive during REM sleep. The overlap of dream imagery and waking consciousness during sleep paralysis can make these episodes particularly vivid and emotionally charged, further emphasizing the role of the brainstem as a regulator caught between two worlds.

Understanding the brainstem's pivotal function not only demystifies sleep paralysis but also underscores the remarkable precision required for seamless transitions between sleep stages. Even minor disruptions in this process can result in profound experiences, highlighting the brainstem's significance in maintaining the boundaries between waking reality and the dream state. Its role in sleep paralysis reveals the complex interplay of neural systems that govern our perceptions and bodily functions, offering insights into one of the brain's most fascinating mechanisms.

The Thalamus and Cortex

The thalamus and cortex play a fascinating duet in the brain's nightly performance, working together to orchestrate the stages of sleep. The thalamus, often described as a sensory gatekeeper, takes on a protective role during non-rapid eye movement (NREM) sleep. It shields the brain from external distractions, effectively blocking out the noise of the waking world. This allows the brain to turn inward, focusing on crucial internal processes like memory consolidation and cellular repair, providing the body and mind with the rest they need.

As the sleep cycle progresses into rapid eye movement (REM) sleep, the dynamic shifts. The thalamus loosens its grip, and the cortex—the outer layer of the brain responsible for higher-level thinking, perception, and imagination—springs to life. This is the playground of dreams, where vivid imagery, intense emotions, and sometimes bizarre narratives unfold. The cortex weaves these dreams with remarkable creativity, drawing on memories, emotions, and even fragments of waking life to construct an alternate reality. It's as though the mind becomes its storyteller, unbound by the constraints of logic or reason.

When sleep paralysis occurs, the intricate balance between the thalamus and cortex is disrupted. Normally, the transition between sleep and wakefulness is smooth, with the thalamus resuming its role as the gatekeeper and the cortex quieting its dream-weaving activity. But in the case of sleep paralysis, part of the brain remains in REM mode while another part awakens. The cortex continues to generate vivid dream-like imagery, but now, these visions overlap with waking consciousness. The result is a surreal and often unsettling experience where the dream world seems to spill into reality.

This blending of states can create incredibly lifelike hallucinations. You might see shadowy figures lurking in the room, feel a strange presence pressing down on your chest, or hear whispers that seem all too real. These sensations are amplified by the brain's emotional centers, which are still highly active from REM sleep. Without the thalamus fully regaining its ability to filter sensory information, the boundary between what is real and imagined becomes blurred, leaving the experiencer in a liminal space that defies logical explanation.

Understanding the roles of the thalamus and cortex sheds light on how such vivid and intense phenomena can occur. It highlights the brain's remarkable complexity—its ability to create entire worlds while dreaming and its capacity to misfire in ways that make those worlds intrude into wakefulness. Sleep paralysis, at its core, is a rare glimpse into the mechanics of the mind, where the barriers between internal and external reality temporarily dissolve. It's a reminder of the delicate balance the brain maintains every night, a dance between dreaming and waking, and how even a brief misstep can create experiences that feel otherworldly.

The Amygdala

The amygdala, a small, almond-shaped structure deep within the brain, is a powerful driver of human emotions, especially fear. It plays a crucial role in assessing potential threats and triggering the body's fight-or-flight response. During REM sleep, the amygdala becomes particularly active, even in the absence of real-world danger. This heightened state of activity reflects the brain's deep engagement with emotionally charged dream content, where fears, anxieties, and other intense feelings are often amplified.

In the context of sleep paralysis, the amygdala's heightened activity becomes a central player in shaping the experience. As the brain lingers in the liminal space between sleep and wakefulness, the vivid imagery and sensations typical of REM sleep spill over into waking awareness. These hallucinations are infused with an emotional intensity that the amygdala generates, often resulting in overwhelming feelings of dread or panic. It's as though the brain's fear circuitry is fully engaged, interpreting the surreal and dream-like elements of sleep paralysis as immediate threats, even when there's no physical danger.

This exaggerated fear response is not random; it's a result of the brain trying to make sense of conflicting signals. The paralysis of the body, the hyper-realistic hallucinations, and the lingering presence of dream logic create a scenario ripe for misinterpretation. The amygdala, operating in overdrive, reacts as if survival is at stake, amplifying sensations and perceptions in a way that feels deeply visceral. This is why even individuals who intellectually understand sleep paralysis often describe an uncontrollable and primal fear during episodes.

The amygdala's role also explains the thematic consistency of many sleep paralysis hallucinations. Reports of shadowy figures, malevolent presences, or feelings of suffocation align with the brain's tendency to interpret ambiguous stimuli through the lens of fear. These archetypal experiences are deeply rooted in the amygdala's function, which has evolved to err on the side of caution in the face of uncertainty. In a state of sleep paralysis, this ancient survival mechanism becomes a source of profound psychological intensity, coloring the experience with a sense of impending doom.

Yet, the amygdala's involvement in sleep paralysis also underscores the deeply emotional nature of these episodes. Fear is a universal language of the brain, and the amygdala's hyperactivity serves as a reminder of how deeply interconnected our emotional and sensory experiences are. It's a vivid demonstration of the brain's capacity to create a world that feels utterly real, shaped not just by external stimuli but by the internal workings of our emotional and instinctual centers. For those who experience sleep paralysis, understanding the amygdala's role can offer a path to reframing fear—not as a signal of real danger but as a reflection of the brain's fascinating and complex inner workings.

Disruptions in Sleep Cycles

Sleep paralysis is often likened to a glitch in the finely tuned system of sleep—a disruption in the seamless transitions that usually govern our nightly rest. But what exactly causes this glitch? To understand, we must delve into the mysterious borderlands of consciousness, those fleeting moments between wakefulness and sleep, where the brain's intricate choreography occasionally stumbles.

These liminal states—known as hypnagogic (when falling asleep) and hypnopompic (when waking up)—serve as the entry and exit points to the dream world. Under normal circumstances, the body and mind transition through these stages in perfect harmony. The body gradually relaxes, and the mind releases its grip on conscious thought, allowing sleep to take hold. Likewise, upon waking, the mind re-engages while the body shakes off its protective paralysis. However, during sleep paralysis, this delicate synchronization falters, leaving the individual suspended between realms.

When sleep paralysis strikes during the hypnagogic state, the body initiates REM sleep prematurely, engaging atonia—the temporary paralysis designed to prevent physical movement during dreams—before the mind fully disengages from wakefulness. Imagine feeling your body sink into the heavy stillness of sleep, only to realize that your mind remains painfully aware. It is as though the door to the dream world has swung open, but your conscious self is still standing on the threshold, unable to step through.

The experience is equally disorienting when sleep paralysis occurs during the hypnopompic state. Here, the reverse scenario unfolds. The mind emerges from the dream state, blinking awake and aware, while the body lags, trapped in atonia. In this unsettling in-between, the sleeper becomes a captive in their own body, fully conscious yet unable to move. This discordant awakening can feel profoundly unnatural as if the machinery of sleep has momentarily betrayed its operator.

These disruptions often bring with them a heightened sense of vulnerability. The body, immobilized and unresponsive, feels like a prison, while the mind, caught in the crossfire of waking and dreaming, struggles to make sense of its surroundings. It is within these moments that the brain, grasping for coherence, may conjure hallucinations—shadowy figures, whispering voices, or the crushing weight of an unseen force. These experiences are not mere figments of imagination but manifestations of a mind caught in the twilight of two worlds, its perception distorted by the clash of biological processes.

What makes these disruptions even more fascinating is their unpredictability. They can be triggered by a variety of factors, from stress and sleep deprivation to irregular schedules or underlying sleep disorders. Yet, despite their capricious nature, they reveal the extraordinary complexity of the sleep cycle—a system so finely tuned that even the smallest misstep can give rise to experiences that feel profoundly otherworldly.

In these fleeting moments of disarray, we glimpse the brain's intricate workings laid bare, its usual harmony replaced by a chaotic dance of overlapping states. Sleep paralysis is not merely a glitch in the system; it is a testament to the fragile balance that underpins one of our most essential and enigmatic functions. To understand it is to peer into the depths of the mind's nightly odyssey, where dreams are born and the boundaries of reality blur.

Case Study: A Fragmented Cycle

Sleep paralysis often strikes during moments of heightened stress or disrupted sleep, as seen in Lila's experience. For many, these episodes serve as an unsettling reminder of the brain's intricate and delicate relationship with rest. Lila's case is a textbook example, but it's far from unique—similar stories reveal how sleep paralysis manifests under varying circumstances, each adding another layer of complexity to our understanding of this phenomenon.

Take Carlos, a paramedic working grueling shifts in a bustling city. The long hours and irregular sleep patterns began to take a toll on his mental and physical health. One night, after a particularly harrowing day at work, Carlos collapsed into bed only to awaken in the middle of the night, unable to move. He described the sensation of an invisible weight pressing on his chest, combined with the terrifying sound of a child's laughter echoing in his ears. "I was wide awake, but I couldn't do anything about it," he recalls. For weeks, the episodes persisted, often accompanied by auditory hallucinations that left him dreading the few hours of sleep he could manage. Carlos eventually sought help from a sleep specialist who identified his irregular sleep cycles as the culprit. By adopting a more structured routine and incorporating mindfulness techniques, Carlos was able to significantly reduce the frequency of his episodes.

Then there's Priya, an artist who found her sleep paralysis episodes intertwined with her creative process. Priya's first encounter occurred during a stressful period when she was working late into the night to meet a gallery deadline. She woke to find herself paralyzed, with the vivid image of a shadowy figure standing at the foot of her bed. Instead of being consumed by fear, Priya began sketching what she saw during her episodes. Her hallucinations evolved into elaborate visions, which she turned into a series of haunting paintings that eventually garnered critical acclaim. "It was terrifying at first, but over time, I started to see it as a strange kind of inspiration," she says. Priya's experience highlights how the mind can transform even distressing phenomena into something meaningful and creative.

Another striking case involves Jamal, a college athlete who started experiencing sleep paralysis after sustaining a concussion during a game. In the weeks following his injury, he began to wake in the middle of the night, unable to move, with a crushing sensation on his chest. During one episode, he swore he could hear his voice calling out to him from a corner of the room. "It felt like my brain was playing tricks on me," he says. A neurologist later explained that his brain's recovery from the concussion likely disrupted his REM cycles, making him more susceptible to sleep paralysis. With time, rest, and physical therapy, Jamal's episodes became less frequent, but they left him with a deeper respect for the complexities of the brain.

Lastly, consider Sarah, a mother of two who began experiencing sleep paralysis after the birth of her second child. Exhausted from sleepless nights and caring for a newborn, Sarah often found herself trapped in bed, unable to move, with the sensation that someone was whispering her name. Her episodes became so frequent that she began to fear going to sleep. Through therapy, Sarah learned that her sleep deprivation and postpartum anxiety were significant contributing factors. Once she started prioritizing self-care and seeking support, her episodes diminished, though the vivid memories of those paralyzed moments still linger.

These stories, each unique yet connected by the common thread of sleep paralysis, offer a window into the human experience of this enigmatic condition. They reveal not only the fragility of the sleep-wake cycle but also the profound psychological impact these episodes can have. Whether terrifying, bewildering, or even inspiring, these experiences remind us of the intricate interplay between the body, mind, and the mysterious realm of sleep.

How the Brain Creates Hallucinations

The human brain is a masterful architect of perception, weaving together sensory input and internal processes to create our experience of reality. Yet, under certain conditions, this delicate balance can falter, giving rise to hallucinations—perceptions without external stimuli. In the context of sleep paralysis, these hallucinations take on an especially vivid and often terrifying quality, blurring the line between the waking world and the dreamscape.

During sleep, the brain enters a complex state where it alternates between different cycles and stages. REM sleep, in particular, is marked by heightened brain activity, akin to wakefulness, but with the body immobilized in a protective paralysis known as atonia. This state allows dreams to unfold without the risk of physical movement. However, when the boundaries between REM sleep and wakefulness blur, the brain can struggle to reconcile these opposing states. The result is a peculiar collision of dream imagery and conscious awareness.

In this liminal state, the brain is still primed for dreaming, even as the sleeper becomes partially awake. Visual and auditory areas of the brain remain active, conjuring vivid images and sounds that feel startlingly real. At the same time, the brain's fear center—the amygdala—often goes into overdrive, interpreting immobility and confusion as signs of danger. This heightened fear response can shape the nature of the hallucinations, giving them a menacing quality that feeds into the sense of vulnerability.

These hallucinations often feel intensely real because the brain uses the same neural pathways to generate them as it does for perceiving the external world. Shadows may morph into ominous figures, whispers may echo in the silence, and the sensation of weight on the chest might be perceived as the grasp of a malevolent presence. For the person experiencing sleep paralysis, the hallucinations are not just fleeting images or sounds; they are immersive, visceral experiences that defy the usual boundaries of reality.

The brain's extraordinary capacity for storytelling plays a crucial role in this phenomenon. It seeks patterns, meaning, and coherence, even in the face of confusion or incomplete information. In the absence of clear sensory input during sleep paralysis, the brain fills the gaps with constructs drawn from memory, culture, and deeply ingrained fears. A person who has heard tales of shadowy intruders or malevolent spirits may find their hallucinations shaped by those narratives, reinforcing the belief in an external threat.

What makes these hallucinations particularly unsettling is their alignment with primal fears—being watched, attacked, or unable to escape. The combination of immobility, heightened sensory awareness, and the brain's fear response creates a perfect storm for generating intensely disturbing experiences. These hallucinations are not merely products of imagination; they are rooted in the brain's fundamental mechanisms for survival, misfiring in a moment of disconnection between sleep and wakefulness.

Despite their terrifying nature, these hallucinations are a testament to the brain's complexity and its tireless effort to make sense of the world, even when caught between states. They reveal the intricate interplay of biology, psychology, and culture, offering a glimpse into the mind's extraordinary capacity to create and interpret reality. For those who experience sleep paralysis, understanding the brain's role in these hallucinations can be a first step toward demystifying the experience and reclaiming a sense of control.

Toward Understanding

By examining the mechanics of sleep, we begin to see how sleep paralysis arises from a complex interplay of biological processes. It is not a curse, a punishment, or a supernatural visitation but a fascinating—albeit unsettling—manifestation of the brain's inner workings.

Yet understanding science is only part of the story. For those who experience sleep paralysis, the knowledge of its physiological roots does not always diminish its impact. The fear, the vividness, and the sense of helplessness remain.

In the next chapter, we will explore how these physiological processes intertwine with psychological and emotional states, delving into the ways that stress, trauma, and mental health influence the occurrence and perception of sleep paralysis.

For now, we rest in the realm of REM, where dreams and paralysis converge—a fragile balance that holds the key to understanding this enigmatic condition.

This chapter provides a deep dive into the scientific foundations of sleep, paving the way for a nuanced exploration of how psychological and emotional factors shape sleep paralysis in the next chapter.

Chapter 6:
The Psychological Dimension of Sleep Paralysis

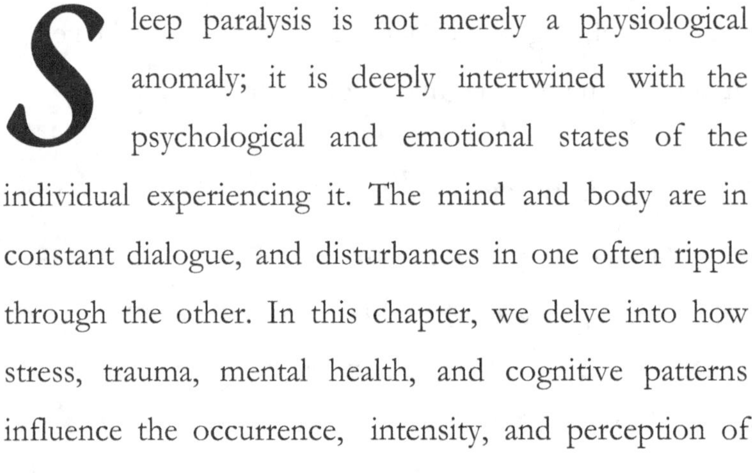

Sleep paralysis is not merely a physiological anomaly; it is deeply intertwined with the psychological and emotional states of the individual experiencing it. The mind and body are in constant dialogue, and disturbances in one often ripple through the other. In this chapter, we delve into how stress, trauma, mental health, and cognitive patterns influence the occurrence, intensity, and perception of sleep paralysis.

The Role of Stress and Anxiety

Stress and anxiety are among the most common triggers for sleep paralysis. When the body is under prolonged stress, the brain's sleep-wake cycle can become disrupted, making the transitions between REM and wakefulness less fluid.

The Biological Connection

Stress activates the hypothalamic-pituitary-adrenal (HPA) axis, increasing the release of cortisol, the body's primary stress hormone. While cortisol levels typically decline in the evening to facilitate sleep, chronic stress can lead to elevated levels at night, delaying or disrupting REM sleep. This irregularity heightens the likelihood of waking during REM atonia, setting the stage for sleep paralysis.

Psychiatrist Dr. Gabriel Singh notes, "When the brain is primed for threat due to stress, sleep paralysis episodes are more likely to be accompanied by fear-laden hallucinations. It's a vicious cycle—the fear amplifies the stress, and the stress increases the frequency of episodes."

Case Study: Stress-Induced Sleep Paralysis

Sophia, a 34-year-old marketing executive, began experiencing sleep paralysis during a particularly demanding period at work. "I'd wake up in the middle of the night, completely frozen. I'd see these shadows moving around my room, and my chest felt like it was being crushed. It got to the point where I was afraid to sleep."

Sophia's sleep study revealed fragmented REM cycles, consistent with stress-induced disturbances. A combination of cognitive-behavioral therapy (CBT) and mindfulness-based stress reduction helped her regain control, reducing both the frequency and intensity of her episodes.

Trauma and Sleep Paralysis

For individuals with a history of trauma, sleep paralysis can become a recurrent and deeply distressing experience. Studies have shown a strong correlation between post-traumatic stress disorder (PTSD) and the frequency of sleep paralysis episodes.

The Hypervigilant Brain

Trauma fundamentally alters the brain, particularly the amygdala, hippocampus, and prefrontal cortex. These changes often result in hypervigilance—a heightened state of alertness to potential threats. This hypervigilance can spill into sleep, making it difficult for the brain to transition smoothly between stages.

Moreover, the fear and helplessness experienced during sleep paralysis can mirror the feelings associated with past trauma, creating a feedback loop that reinforces both.

The Intersection of Trauma and Hallucinations

Hallucinations during sleep paralysis often draw on the individual's subconscious fears. For trauma survivors, these fears can be particularly vivid and personal. A veteran who has PTSD, for example, might experience sleep paralysis as the sensation of being pinned down or attacked, mirroring the physical constraints of a traumatic event.

Mental Health and Sleep Paralysis

The relationship between mental health and sleep paralysis is a fascinating and intricate one, revealing how deeply our emotional and psychological states influence the body's delicate balance during sleep. Sleep paralysis, often described as a collision between the dream state and waking reality, can be profoundly shaped by underlying mental health conditions. These conditions affect not only how often episodes occur but also the intensity and nature of the experiences.

Anxiety, one of the most pervasive mental health challenges, is strongly linked to sleep paralysis. The relentless cycle of worry and hyperarousal that defines anxiety disorders primes the brain to remain on high alert, even during rest. This state of heightened vigilance can disrupt normal sleep patterns, making the transitions between sleep stages more erratic. When the brain struggles to move seamlessly from REM sleep to wakefulness, the conditions for sleep paralysis are set. For those with anxiety, this experience can be particularly harrowing, as the hyperactive fear response amplifies the perceived threat of hallucinations or the sensation of paralysis itself.

Depression also plays a significant role in sleep paralysis. The altered neurochemical environment associated with depression, particularly changes in serotonin and dopamine levels, impacts the brain's sleep-wake regulation. People with depression often experience fragmented or shallow sleep, which increases the likelihood of disturbances in REM sleep. Sleep paralysis episodes in individuals with depression may carry a distinct emotional weight, with hallucinations reflecting feelings of despair, helplessness, or isolation. The paralysis may feel less like a temporary glitch and more like a physical manifestation of the emotional stagnation and heaviness that depression brings.

Bipolar disorder adds another layer of complexity to the connection between mental health and sleep paralysis.

The dramatic mood shifts that characterize this condition—oscillating between manic highs and depressive lows—can wreak havoc on sleep architecture. During manic phases, a reduced need for sleep and heightened energy disrupt normal REM cycles, while depressive phases often bring hypersomnia or poor sleep quality. These irregularities in sleep patterns make people with bipolar disorder particularly susceptible to the kind of neurological misfires that trigger sleep paralysis. The content of these episodes may even mirror the emotional extremes of the disorder, shifting between exhilarating or grandiose hallucinations during manic phases and terrifying or oppressive ones during depressive phases.

Trauma, too, leaves its mark on sleep paralysis. For individuals with post-traumatic stress disorder (PTSD), the brain's attempts to process deeply embedded fears and memories during REM sleep can overflow into waking consciousness. The heightened amygdala activity typical of trauma survivors can intensify the fear and vividness of hallucinations, often intertwining them with elements of past traumatic experiences. For someone with PTSD, sleep paralysis is not merely a disorienting episode—it becomes a replay of unresolved fear, underscoring the profound impact of trauma on both the waking and sleeping mind.

The connection between mental health and sleep paralysis isn't solely about pathology, though. It also highlights the extraordinary sensitivity of the human brain to the interplay of emotions, thoughts, and physical states. Sleep paralysis acts as a mirror, reflecting the inner workings of the psyche in a way that is both revealing and unsettling. For those grappling with mental health challenges, these episodes can feel like an intrusion of their struggles into the sanctuary of sleep, a place meant for rest and renewal.

Understanding the role of mental health in sleep paralysis is vital, not only for finding ways to cope but for appreciating the profound interconnectedness of mind and body. It reminds us that sleep is far more than a passive state—it is a dynamic process deeply entwined with our emotional and psychological well-being. While the experience of sleep paralysis can be frightening, it also offers a unique window into the workings of the brain, providing insights into how deeply our mental health shapes every aspect of our existence, even in our most vulnerable moments of rest.

Anxiety Disorders

Anxiety disorders and sleep paralysis form a complex and deeply interconnected relationship, one that highlights the profound ways in which our emotional states influence even the most fundamental processes of rest and recovery. Anxiety, with its hallmark of heightened arousal and an overactive fear response, creates a fertile ground for the unsettling symptoms of sleep paralysis to thrive. For individuals living with conditions like generalized anxiety disorder (GAD) or panic disorder, the experience of sleep paralysis can feel especially overwhelming, as their minds are already primed to sense danger and amplify perceived threats.

At its core, anxiety keeps the brain on high alert, scanning the environment—real or imagined—for signs of harm. This heightened vigilance, though adaptive in certain contexts, becomes maladaptive when it interferes with the body's natural rhythms, including sleep. Anxiety often disrupts the depth and quality of rest, fragmenting sleep cycles and increasing the likelihood of disturbances during transitions between stages, particularly during the vulnerable state of REM sleep. When the body attempts to wake while still under the neurological grip of REM atonia, the result is paralysis and vivid hallucinations that define sleep paralysis.

For someone with anxiety, these episodes can feel like a cruel extension of their waking struggles. The inability to move, combined with the vivid and often terrifying hallucinations, can feel like confirmation of their worst fears. A shadowy figure looming in the room might not be interpreted as a harmless illusion but as an imminent and tangible threat. For those with panic disorder, the experience can trigger a full-blown panic response, complete with a racing heart, shallow breathing, and an overwhelming sense of impending doom—all while being trapped in a body that refuses to respond.

The emotional landscape of sleep paralysis for an anxious mind is uniquely intense. Fear, already heightened by the disorder, becomes magnified in the paralysis state, where the normal boundaries between dream logic and waking reality blur. The brain's hyperactive amygdala, responsible for processing fear, plays a central role in these episodes. It feeds the hallucinations with emotional intensity, creating scenarios that feel viscerally real—whether it's a looming sense of suffocation, the presence of malevolent entities, or the inexplicable weight pressing down on the chest.

What makes the experience even more challenging is how it can reinforce the cycle of anxiety. A single terrifying episode of sleep paralysis might lead to a lingering fear of sleep itself, creating a vicious loop where anxiety about the next occurrence disrupts rest, making future episodes more likely. For someone already wrestling with anxiety's grip during the day, the idea of sleep, meant to be a time of restoration, becomes yet another source of stress.

Yet, within this unsettling interplay lies an opportunity for understanding. Sleep paralysis offers a visceral glimpse into how anxiety shapes perception, often transforming neutral stimuli into perceived threats. For those willing to approach the phenomenon with curiosity rather than fear, it can become a doorway to greater self-awareness. Techniques such as mindfulness and controlled breathing, often used in anxiety management, can be particularly effective during sleep paralysis episodes. While they don't immediately dispel the paralysis, they can shift the experiencer's focus away from fear and toward calm, breaking the hold of panic.

The connection between anxiety disorders and sleep paralysis serves as a reminder of the deep ties between mind and body. It underscores how emotional states, particularly those as pervasive as anxiety, ripple through every aspect of our being, shaping not only how we perceive the world but how we experience our internal landscapes. While sleep paralysis can be a frightening encounter, understanding its roots in anxiety provides a path toward reclaiming a sense of control, even in the most vulnerable moments. It's a reminder that while fear may loom large at the moment, it is not insurmountable—and that both the waking and dreaming mind have the capacity for resilience and growth.

Depression

Depression weaves its influence into nearly every aspect of life, including the intricate workings of the sleep-wake cycle. Sleep, which should serve as a refuge, often becomes a battleground for those living with depression. One of the most significant disruptions depression causes is in the regulation of REM sleep, the stage where dreaming is most vivid and the brain is most active. For many individuals with depression, the body enters REM earlier in the sleep cycle than it typically would—a phenomenon known as reduced REM latency. This irregularity not only disturbs the restorative balance of sleep but also heightens the risk of experiencing sleep paralysis, particularly during those fragile moments of early morning awakenings when the body and mind are caught between states.

The interplay between depression and sleep paralysis is profound and multifaceted. Depression already imposes a heavy toll on the mind, often characterized by feelings of helplessness, persistent fatigue, and an overwhelming sense of being trapped in one's thoughts. Sleep paralysis mirrors these sensations in an almost eerie fashion, creating an experience that feels like an extension of depression itself. The immobilization of the body during an episode can evoke the same sense of being stuck, powerless to break free, that is so familiar to those grappling with depressive thoughts.

What makes this connection even more intense is the way depression amplifies the emotional weight of sleep paralysis episodes. The hallucinations that often accompany paralysis—shadowy figures, oppressive sensations, or an inexplicable sense of doom—take on a more sinister quality when filtered through the lens of depression. The mind, already predisposed to interpret experiences in a negative or fatalistic way, may imbue these episodes with a heightened sense of dread or despair. A fleeting moment of paralysis can linger in the psyche, feeding the cycle of fear, disrupted sleep, and emotional exhaustion.

The timing of sleep paralysis during early morning awakenings is particularly striking in the context of depression. The early morning hours are often fraught with difficulty for those living with this condition, as they can bring a sharp contrast between the hopefulness of a new day and the heaviness of depressive thoughts. Waking into paralysis during this time can feel like a cruel trick of the mind and body, blurring the boundaries between dreams and waking life in a way that exacerbates feelings of vulnerability.

Yet, the relationship between depression and sleep paralysis also offers insight into the profound ways in which mental health shapes our experiences of the physical world. Depression's impact on REM sleep reflects the deep entanglement of emotional states and physiological processes, showing how the brain's attempt to navigate imbalance can manifest in both dreams and wakefulness. For those who experience both conditions, this interplay can provide an opportunity to better understand the connections between their mental health and their sleep patterns, offering a path to healing that encompasses both mind and body.

The complexity of depression's relationship with sleep paralysis underscores the need for compassion, both toward oneself and from others. These episodes, though distressing, can serve as a reminder of the brain's intricate workings and its capacity to signal when something deeper needs attention. For those willing to explore the roots of these experiences, sleep paralysis can become more than just a frightening anomaly; it can become a window into the mind's struggle and a step toward addressing the underlying challenges.

In the broader picture, depression and sleep paralysis highlight the fragility and resilience of the human experience. They reveal how deeply intertwined our emotional and physical worlds are, how disruptions in one can cascade into the other, and how even the most disconcerting phenomena can hold the potential for greater understanding. For those navigating both conditions, the path may be difficult. Still, it is also one of discovery, reminding us of the importance of care, reflection, and the pursuit of balance in the face of life's complexities.

Bipolar Disorder

Bipolar disorder adds a layer of complexity to the experience of sleep paralysis, intertwining erratic mood states with the delicate mechanisms of sleep. For individuals living with bipolar disorder, the unpredictable shifts between depressive, manic, and mixed episodes create an environment where sleep patterns are frequently disrupted. This disruption extends beyond simple insomnia or hypersomnia; it affects the intricate transitions the brain must navigate during the sleep cycle. Sleep paralysis often emerges in this context, as the brain struggles to maintain seamless coordination between the physical and mental states that define restful sleep.

During depressive or mixed episodes, when feelings of despair or agitation dominate, the likelihood of sleep paralysis seems to increase. These mood states often bring about fragmented sleep, where periods of rest are shallow, interrupted, or inconsistent. The brain's struggle to enter or exit the deeper stages of sleep with precision creates a perfect storm for paralysis. The boundaries between wakefulness and dreaming blur, leaving the individual caught in a distressing state of partial awareness where the body feels trapped, unresponsive, and vulnerable.

The emotional landscape of bipolar disorder intensifies the experience of sleep paralysis. Hallucinations during these episodes—whether visual, auditory, or tactile—often mirror the heightened emotional states associated with bipolar disorder. For someone in a depressive episode, these hallucinations might take on a bleak, oppressive tone, amplifying feelings of hopelessness or fear. Conversely, during a mixed episode where agitation and despair coexist, the hallucinations might feel chaotic or overwhelming, compounding the sense of being unable to escape both the paralysis and the emotional turmoil.

What makes sleep paralysis particularly challenging for individuals with bipolar disorder is how closely it aligns with the disorder's cycles of dysregulation. In mania, the need for sleep diminishes, often leading to prolonged periods of wakefulness that throw off the body's internal rhythms. When the cycle inevitably shifts back toward depression or a mixed state, the cumulative effects of disrupted sleep begin to take their toll. Sleep paralysis, in this context, becomes not just a physiological phenomenon but a reflection of the underlying instability that bipolar disorder creates within the body and mind.

Despite its unsettling nature, the link between bipolar disorder and sleep paralysis offers a deeper understanding of how mental health and sleep are intricately connected. The brain's mechanisms for managing mood, energy, and sleep are deeply intertwined, and any disruption in one area inevitably affects the others. Sleep paralysis, while distressing, serves as a signal of this imbalance, highlighting the need for care in managing the disorder holistically. Stable sleep patterns, though challenging to achieve in the face of bipolar disorder, can significantly reduce the frequency of these episodes, offering some relief.

For those navigating both bipolar disorder and sleep paralysis, the experience can feel overwhelming, as if the mind and body are conspiring to keep peace and rest just out of reach. However, recognizing the connections between mood regulation, sleep architecture, and these episodes can be empowering. By addressing the root causes of sleep disruption—whether through therapy, medication, or lifestyle adjustments—individuals can begin to regain some control over their experiences.

Ultimately, the interplay between bipolar disorder and sleep paralysis underscores the complexity of the human mind. It reminds us of the importance of understanding how emotional states influence physical experiences and vice versa. While sleep paralysis is a challenging aspect of living with bipolar disorder, it also serves as a testament to the resilience of those who face these struggles daily, working tirelessly to navigate a condition that touches every facet of their being.

Cognitive Patterns and Perception

The way we perceive and interpret sleep paralysis has an undeniable impact on how we experience it. Our thoughts, beliefs, and cognitive patterns can either soothe or intensify the fear and distress that often accompany these episodes. The mind plays a powerful role in shaping the narrative of sleep paralysis, and this narrative, in turn, influences how the body and emotions respond to the experience.

For many, the immediate reaction to sleep paralysis is fear—a deeply ingrained response to the sudden loss of control over one's body. This fear is often compounded by cognitive distortions, those irrational or exaggerated patterns of thinking that lead the mind down a spiraling path of worst-case scenarios. Thoughts like *"I'm being attacked by something malevolent"* or *"This will never end"* can transform a fleeting episode into an overwhelming ordeal. These mental scripts, born from the brain's natural tendency to seek explanations for the unknown, often draw on personal fears or cultural narratives about the supernatural, turning a physiological phenomenon into a psychological battlefield.

The power of interpretation is especially evident in the way hallucinations are experienced during sleep paralysis. If the mind is primed to see the unknown as threatening, the brain will often project those fears into the experience. A shadowy figure becomes an intruder; an ambiguous sound becomes an ominous whisper. These perceptions, though vivid and seemingly real, are amplified by the lens through which the mind views them. Cognitive patterns shape not only what we feel but also how we remember and anticipate future episodes, creating a feedback loop that can either heighten or diminish the distress.

Interestingly, individuals who approach sleep paralysis with curiosity or neutrality often report less fear and more curiosity, even in the face of similar sensory phenomena. This difference highlights how much influence perception holds over experience. By shifting thoughts away from catastrophic interpretations and toward a more grounded understanding— such as viewing paralysis as a temporary and natural misstep in the sleep process—individuals can reduce the intensity of their fear. Recognizing the experience for what it is can help break the cycle of terror, allowing for a calmer, more manageable encounter.

For those prone to cognitive distortions, understanding their influence on sleep paralysis can be transformative. Simple awareness of the mind's tendency to catastrophize or magnify fears can act as a first step toward reclaiming control. Techniques like mindfulness, which encourages observing thoughts without attaching to them, or cognitive-behavioral strategies, which challenge irrational beliefs, can help reframe the experience. Over time, these approaches can replace fear-driven narratives with ones that are more rational and less overwhelming.

Our thoughts and perceptions do not operate in isolation—they are shaped by personal experiences, cultural beliefs, and even the stories we hear from others. Sleep paralysis, often portrayed in folklore or media as something dark and malevolent inherits much of this cultural baggage. These narratives become part of the mental framework through which we interpret the phenomenon, coloring our perceptions and amplifying distress. Breaking free from these ingrained beliefs can be challenging but essential in reshaping the experience into something less threatening.

The interplay between cognition and sleep paralysis is a testament to the mind's power to influence reality. What we believe, expect, and focus on can transform a brief, physiological event into something profound and, at times, terrifying. Yet, this same power can be harnessed to create a sense of understanding and even empowerment. By exploring the thoughts that arise during and after episodes, individuals can begin to rewrite the story of their experience, taking it from one of fear and helplessness to one of curiosity and resilience.

Catastrophizing

A common cognitive distortion in sleep paralysis is catastrophizing, where individuals assume the worst possible outcome. For example, someone might believe that the shadowy figure they see is a real intruder or that the inability to breathe will lead to suffocation.

Hyperfocus on the Experience

Focusing excessively on the fear or discomfort during sleep paralysis can intensify the emotional response, creating a self-reinforcing cycle. Psychologists often encourage individuals to adopt grounding techniques or cognitive reframing to disrupt this cycle.

Cognitive Reframing in Action

One technique involves reframing the experience as a harmless neurological glitch rather than a supernatural or life-threatening event. "When I started telling myself, 'This is just my brain playing tricks on me,' it changed everything," says Marcus, a 41-year-old software engineer. "I still had episodes, but they didn't scare me as much."

Sleep Paralysis as a Window into the Mind

While sleep paralysis is undeniably distressing, some researchers view it as an opportunity to explore the unconscious mind. The vivid hallucinations and heightened emotions offer a rare glimpse into the interplay between waking cognition and dream states.

Lucid Dreaming and Sleep Paralysis

Sleep paralysis, though often associated with fear and helplessness, can hold an unexpected allure for those brave enough to explore its depths. For some, this state serves as an entry point into lucid dreaming, where the dreamer becomes fully aware that they are dreaming and can often steer the course of their nocturnal adventures. It's a unique and transformative opportunity, turning an otherwise unsettling experience into one of discovery, creativity, and even joy.

The connection between sleep paralysis and lucid dreaming lies in their shared liminal nature—both exist in the delicate space between waking and sleeping. During sleep paralysis, the body remains in a state of atonia, the muscle inhibition of REM sleep, while the mind flits between consciousness and the dream world. This overlap creates a unique window where the dreamer can step into a lucid state. The paralysis itself, rather than being a barrier, becomes a kind of bridge—one that requires courage and a calm mind to cross.

The fear that often accompanies sleep paralysis can act as a formidable obstacle. Still, those who learn to manage it find themselves in a position to shift the experience into something more empowering. This shift begins with reframing the experience: understanding that the terrifying sensations are products of the brain's hypnagogic state rather than real threats. Breathing deeply, maintaining a sense of curiosity, and reminding oneself of the temporary nature of the episode are tools that can ease the transition from paralysis into lucidity.

Once fear is mastered, the possibilities become exhilarating. Imagine realizing you are in a dream, able to shape its landscapes, characters, and events according to your will. Some describe the experience as stepping into an infinite canvas where the rules of reality dissolve. Dreamers have flown through fantastical worlds, met with symbolic figures, or delved into personal memories for insight and healing—all starting from the stillness of sleep paralysis.

Dr. Elena Morales, a psychologist and dream researcher, emphasizes the psychological potential of this transition. "Sleep paralysis sits at the boundary between consciousness and the dream world. For individuals willing to explore that boundary, it can open doors to incredible creative and psychological insights." This dual awareness of being awake and dreaming grants an unparalleled level of control and reflection, blending the emotional intensity of dreams with the clarity of a waking mind.

There's also a deeply personal and transformative quality to lucid dreaming initiated through sleep paralysis. The act of overcoming fear to access a richer dream experience can have ripple effects in waking life, fostering confidence, emotional resilience, and a willingness to confront the unknown. For many, the journey through paralysis into lucidity mirrors broader personal challenges—the ability to face inner fears and emerge stronger, more aware, and more connected to oneself.

The interplay of lucidity and sleep paralysis is not just about escaping terror but about embracing the full spectrum of human experience. Dreams offer a unique space where the conscious and subconscious mind meet, and sleep paralysis can be the portal to that realm. It's a reminder that even the most unsettling moments hold within them the seeds of wonder, creativity, and transformation.

Personal Empowerment

Reframing sleep paralysis as an opportunity rather than a threat can be transformative. Some individuals report using episodes as a form of exposure therapy, gradually reducing their fear through repeated encounters with the phenomenon.

The Intersection of Science and Experience

Understanding the psychological dimensions of sleep paralysis is essential for both individuals and clinicians. It is not enough to explain the phenomenon through biology alone; we must also address the emotional and cognitive impact it has on those who experience it.

As we move into the next chapter, we will explore the role of culture in shaping the narratives and interpretations of sleep paralysis, examining how beliefs, traditions, and societal norms influence the way people perceive and cope with this mysterious condition.

For now, we leave the realm of the individual psyche, stepping into the broader context of collective human experience, where psychology and culture converge.

This chapter dives deeply into the psychological factors influencing sleep paralysis, blending clinical insights with personal narratives to create a comprehensive exploration.

Chapter 7:

Common Triggers

Sleep paralysis, while mysterious, often emerges from identifiable patterns rooted in daily habits, mental health, and environmental factors. Understanding the triggers behind this phenomenon can provide not only a sense of control for those affected but also a roadmap for prevention. Many who experience sleep paralysis may find the episodes unpredictable, but closer examination often reveals common culprits like irregular sleep patterns, stress, substance use, and mental health challenges. These triggers, woven into the fabric of modern life, play a significant role in disrupting the delicate balance of the brain's sleep mechanisms.

One of the most pervasive triggers is irregular sleep schedules. The human body thrives on routine, guided by the circadian rhythm—a natural internal clock that governs sleep and wake cycles. When disrupted, whether due to shift work, jet lag, or inconsistent bedtime habits, this rhythm falters. For instance, Lisa, a nurse working rotating night shifts, began experiencing sleep paralysis after years of erratic schedules. Her episodes typically followed nights when she struggled to adjust her body clock to a new shift. "It was like my brain and body were out of sync," she explained. Clinical studies support her experience, showing that irregular sleep can fragment REM cycles, creating the perfect storm for sleep paralysis to occur.

Stress, another ubiquitous aspect of life, is a significant contributor to sleep paralysis. The brain, under constant strain, often struggles to transition smoothly between sleep stages. Take Mark, a college student navigating the pressures of exams, internships, and financial concerns. During one particularly stressful semester, he began waking in the middle of the night, unable to move and convinced someone was standing in his room. "It was the most helpless feeling I've ever had," Mark recalls. Stress hormones like cortisol can interfere with sleep quality, heightening the likelihood of fragmented REM cycles where sleep paralysis thrives.

Substance use, particularly alcohol and stimulants, further exacerbates the risk. While alcohol may initially induce drowsiness, it disrupts the natural progression of sleep stages, particularly REM sleep. Emily, a graphic designer, noticed her episodes were more frequent after nights of heavy drinking. "At first, I thought it was just bad dreams," she said, "but then I realized it only happened after late nights out." Stimulants like caffeine or recreational drugs similarly throw the brain's sleep architecture into disarray, often leading to a heightened susceptibility to sleep paralysis.

Mental health conditions, such as anxiety and depression, also play a crucial role. These disorders can distort sleep patterns, making it harder for the brain to navigate the boundaries between wakefulness and sleep. Julia, who had struggled with generalized anxiety for years, found that her episodes often coincided with periods of heightened worry. "It felt like my mind couldn't fully turn off, even when my body was exhausted," she shared. Research shows a strong correlation between sleep paralysis and mental health conditions, suggesting that addressing underlying psychological issues may help reduce episodes.

Real-life scenarios further illustrate the multifaceted nature of these triggers. Consider Daniel, a software engineer who began experiencing sleep paralysis during a particularly demanding project at work. His episodes coincided with late nights, excessive caffeine intake, and mounting stress from looming deadlines. "It was like my body was trying to shut down, but my brain refused," he explained. After seeking advice from a sleep specialist, Daniel adopted a more structured sleep routine and cut back on stimulants, leading to a significant reduction in episodes.

Clinical studies have shed light on effective strategies to mitigate these triggers. Consistency in sleep schedules, stress management techniques like meditation or therapy, and reducing substance use can significantly decrease the likelihood of experiencing sleep paralysis. Maintaining good sleep hygiene—such as creating a calming bedtime routine, limiting screen time before bed, and ensuring a comfortable sleep environment—further supports the brain's ability to transition smoothly between sleep stages.

These insights highlight the importance of recognizing and addressing the common triggers of sleep paralysis. While the experience itself can be deeply unsettling, understanding its roots offers a pathway to prevention and empowerment. By making deliberate changes to daily habits and seeking support when needed, individuals can regain control over their sleep and, in turn, their peace of mind.

Chapter 8:
Sleep Paralysis Through History

Throughout history, humanity has sought to explain and contextualize the strange and often terrifying phenomenon of sleep paralysis. Ancient texts, religious doctrines, and medical treatises reveal how various civilizations grappled with its enigma, offering explanations that ranged from divine intervention to demonic attack. This chapter explores the historical interpretations of sleep paralysis, tracing its evolution from mystical encounters to a subject of scientific inquiry.

Ancient Civilizations and Divine Encounters

In ancient civilizations, sleep paralysis was woven into the fabric of spiritual and religious life, often seen as a moment of divine connection or confrontation. These episodes, with their vivid imagery and intense emotions, were not dismissed as mere dreams but embraced as encounters with gods, spirits, or other supernatural forces. Many believed that during sleep paralysis, the soul traversed unseen realms, granting glimpses of higher truths or messages from the divine.

In some cultures, the inability to move was interpreted as the presence of a powerful deity or spirit, its overwhelming energy rendering the body immobile. Such experiences were often regarded as sacred, a moment when the mortal and the divine intersected. These narratives brought both awe and reverence as individuals sought to decode the symbolic meanings of their encounters.

Rather than sources of fear alone, these episodes were often celebrated as spiritual tests or opportunities for enlightenment. Rituals, prayers, and sacred ceremonies were developed to honor or appease the forces believed to be involved, underscoring how deeply these experiences shaped ancient understandings of the human connection to the cosmos.

The Egyptian Perspective

The Egyptian perspective on sleep paralysis is steeped in a rich tapestry of mythology, religion, and cultural beliefs that intertwine the natural and supernatural. In ancient Egypt, sleep and dreams were seen as liminal states, bridges between the mortal world and the divine or the realm of spirits. Sleep paralysis, though not named or scientifically understood in antiquity, would likely have been interpreted within this mystical framework.

Egyptians believed that the soul, or *ba*, could travel outside the body during sleep, wandering the spiritual planes. This belief aligned with their understanding of dreams as messages from gods or encounters with the deceased. Sleep paralysis episodes, where individuals awoke unable to move and often sensed a threatening presence, might have been interpreted as the soul encountering obstacles during its nocturnal journey or being restrained by malevolent forces. The sensation of pressure on the chest, so common in sleep paralysis, might have been attributed to an attack by a supernatural entity or the presence of a restless spirit.

The ancient Egyptians also had a complex pantheon of gods and spirits, many of whom played roles in protecting or afflicting the human soul. For instance, the goddess Hathor was associated with dreams and sleep, offering comfort and guidance. Conversely, malevolent spirits or deities such as Ammut, the devourer of the unjust, were believed to prey upon the wicked or those who had not lived a virtuous life. A sleep paralysis episode could easily have been seen as a warning or punishment from these divine or spiritual entities.

Interestingly, the ancient Egyptians placed great importance on the heart as the seat of the soul and conscience. This belief might explain why sensations of chest pressure during sleep paralysis were considered significant. The pressure could have been interpreted as a literal or symbolic burden, perhaps reflecting unresolved guilt, divine judgment, or a spiritual imbalance. Remedies for such experiences would have likely involved rituals, prayers, or the use of protective amulets designed to ward off evil and restore harmony between the body and soul.

One key figure in Egyptian spirituality was the scribe and god Thoth, associated with wisdom, writing, and magic. Thoth was believed to have power over the dream world and could offer protection during sleep. Those who experienced troubling dreams or sleep paralysis might have sought the aid of Thoth through incantations or inscriptions on papyrus designed to shield the dreamer from harm.

The Egyptian concept of the afterlife and its trials also influenced interpretations of sleep paralysis. The journey to the afterlife involved navigating various challenges, some of which were described as encounters with terrifying beings or entities. A sleep paralysis episode, with its accompanying hallucinations, might have been seen as a preview or reflection of these challenges, urging the individual to prepare their soul for the afterlife by living a righteous and spiritually attuned life.

Despite the supernatural framing, the ancient Egyptians were also astute observers of the natural world and their bodies. They recognized the importance of balance and health, which extended to their understanding of sleep. Insomnia, nightmares, and other disturbances were taken seriously and addressed through a combination of medical, spiritual, and magical practices. Remedies for sleep disturbances, including sleep paralysis, often involved herbal treatments, purification rituals, and invoking protective deities to ensure peaceful rest.

In modern Egypt, echoes of these ancient beliefs persist in cultural narratives about sleep and the supernatural. Sleep paralysis is sometimes attributed to *jinn*, spirits from Islamic tradition, who are thought to cause disturbances in vulnerable individuals. While the lens has shifted from ancient Egyptian gods to Islamic cosmology, the core idea remains sleep paralysis is a moment of vulnerability where the physical and spiritual worlds intersect.

This enduring connection between sleep, the soul, and spiritual forces highlights the deep and multifaceted ways in which the Egyptian perspective on sleep paralysis has evolved over millennia, reflecting both the continuity of cultural beliefs and their adaptation to new religious and scientific paradigms.

Ancient Greek and Roman Interpretations

The Greeks and Romans often associated sleep paralysis with the activities of supernatural beings. In Greek mythology, *Ephialtes*, a demon-like figure, was said to descend upon sleeping individuals, causing them to feel suffocated. The word *Ephialtes* eventually became synonymous with nightmares in ancient Greek.

Roman writers such as Pliny the Elder and Galen also wrote about nocturnal disturbances resembling sleep paralysis, though their interpretations varied. Galen, a prominent physician, suggested a physiological basis, attributing the phenomenon to indigestion or poor humoral balance.

The Middle Ages: Demonology and Witchcraft

During the Middle Ages, sleep paralysis became inextricably linked with the belief in demons and witchcraft. The fear of malevolent forces was pervasive, and the symptoms of sleep paralysis often aligned with descriptions of demonic possession or supernatural attack.

The Incubus and Succubus

Medieval folklore described encounters with incubus and succubus demons—male and female spirits, respectively, that would prey on sleeping individuals. Victims often reported sensations of paralysis, pressure on the chest, and vivid sexual imagery, closely mirroring modern accounts of sleep paralysis.

Witchcraft Trials

The witchcraft trials in Europe further entwined sleep paralysis with supernatural explanations. Accusations of witchcraft often included testimony from individuals who claimed to have been paralyzed or tormented by witches during the night. In some cases, the hallucinations experienced during sleep paralysis were presented as evidence of witchcraft, leading to severe repercussions for the accused.

The Renaissance and Early Scientific Inquiry

The Renaissance marked a shift toward more naturalistic explanations for sleep paralysis as thinkers began to challenge supernatural interpretations with emerging scientific principles.

The Writings of Paracelsus

Swiss physician and alchemist Paracelsus was among the first to propose a medical explanation for sleep paralysis. He described it as a disorder caused by an imbalance of bodily humor, rejecting the notion of demonic possession. While his theories were still rudimentary, they represented an important step toward understanding sleep paralysis as a physical phenomenon.

The Influence of the Enlightenment

The Enlightenment further encouraged skepticism of supernatural explanations, emphasizing reason and empirical evidence. Sleep paralysis began to be discussed in medical texts as a neurological or psychological condition. This shift laid the groundwork for modern sleep science, although cultural and religious interpretations persisted in many regions.

The 19th Century: Bridging Myth and Medicine

The 19th century saw the coexistence of folklore and medical inquiry as advancements in neurology and psychology began to shed light on sleep paralysis.

Charles Dickens and the Literary Connection

In his 1836 work *The Pickwick Papers*, Charles Dickens described symptoms resembling sleep paralysis in a character suffering from a "nightmare." The vivid portrayal reflects both the growing awareness of the phenomenon and its persistent association with fear and dread.

Medical Advances

Neurologists and psychiatrists of the 19th century began to document sleep paralysis in greater detail, often linking it to conditions such as narcolepsy, epilepsy, or hysteria. Jean-Martin Charcot, the father of modern neurology, studied cases of sleep paralysis in the context of his work on neurological disorders, emphasizing its physiological basis.

The 20th Century: Modern Science Takes Hold

The 20th century marked a turning point in the understanding of sleep paralysis with the development of sleep medicine and advances in neuroscience.

The Discovery of REM Sleep

In the 1950s, researchers Nathaniel Kleitman and Eugene Aserinsky discovered rapid eye movement (REM) sleep, a breakthrough that revolutionized the study of sleep disorders. Sleep paralysis was identified as a disruption of the REM cycle, where the brain awakens while the body remains in a state of atonia (muscle paralysis).

The Rise of Sleep Clinics

The establishment of sleep clinics in the latter half of the century provided a platform for systematic research on sleep paralysis. Researchers began to categorize it as a parasomnia and explored its relationship with conditions like narcolepsy and anxiety disorders.

Cultural Retention of Myth

Despite scientific advancements, cultural and spiritual interpretations of sleep paralysis persisted, particularly in non-Western societies. In some cases, traditional and modern explanations merged, with individuals attributing episodes to both physiological and supernatural causes.

Sleep Paralysis in the 21st Century

The 21st century has seen an explosion of interest in sleep paralysis fueled by the internet, popular media, and interdisciplinary research.

The Role of Technology

Online forums and social media platforms have allowed individuals to share their experiences of sleep paralysis, creating a global community. While this has increased awareness and reduced stigma, it has also perpetuated myths and sensationalized accounts.

Interdisciplinary Approaches

Modern research on sleep paralysis integrates neuroscience, psychology, and cultural anthropology, reflecting its multifaceted nature. Scientists continue to investigate the neural mechanisms underlying the phenomenon, while cultural scholars examine its significance in various societies.

A Historical Legacy

The history of sleep paralysis is a testament to humanity's enduring quest to understand the unknown. From divine encounters to neurological explanations, each era's interpretation reflects its prevailing worldview, offering insights into the interplay between science, culture, and belief.

As we move into the next chapter, we will explore the neurological underpinnings of sleep paralysis, delving into the brain's intricate processes and how they contribute to this fascinating phenomenon. For now, we pause to reflect on the rich tapestry of history that has shaped our understanding of sleep paralysis, bridging the ancient and the modern, the mystical and the scientific.

Chapter 9:
The Neurological Symphony of Sleep Paralysis

The neuroscience behind the hallucinations experienced during sleep paralysis is a fascinating interplay of brain activity and perception, highlighting how the mind can generate vivid, sometimes terrifying, imagery without external stimuli. At the heart of this phenomenon is the unique state of the brain during sleep paralysis, caught between wakefulness and REM sleep. This transitional phase creates a perfect storm for hallucinations to arise, as the mechanisms regulating sleep and consciousness temporarily overlap in unexpected ways.

During REM sleep, the brain is highly active, particularly in regions associated with emotions, memories, and sensory processing. The amygdala, a structure responsible for processing fear and emotional responses, becomes especially active. In the safety of a normal dream, this heightened activity might manifest as dramatic or emotionally charged dream scenarios. However, in sleep paralysis, the boundaries between the dream state and waking consciousness blur. The individual is aware of their surroundings yet unable to move, and the hyperactive amygdala often generates feelings of intense fear or a sense of an ominous presence nearby. This misfiring of the fear response is why hallucinations during sleep paralysis are frequently described as menacing or threatening.

Visual and auditory hallucinations are common during these episodes, a result of heightened activity in the brain's sensory processing centers. The visual cortex may generate images that are projected into the waking environment, such as shadowy figures or indistinct shapes looming nearby. Similarly, the auditory cortex can create sounds—whispers, footsteps, or even screams—that feel as real as anything heard in the waking world. These hallucinations are not mere remnants of dreams; they are a unique product of the brain's attempt to reconcile conflicting signals from its sensory and cognitive systems.

Tactile hallucinations add another layer of complexity. Many individuals report sensations of pressure on their chest as if being held down or suffocated. This sensation can be traced to the brain's interpretation of atonia, the temporary paralysis that prevents physical movement during REM sleep. With the body immobilized, the mind may interpret paralysis as external force or pressure. This misinterpretation is compounded by the brain's tendency to seek explanations for unusual experiences, often drawing on deeply ingrained fears or cultural narratives to make sense of the sensations.

Interestingly, sleep paralysis hallucinations are not entirely arbitrary. They often reflect universal themes that resonate across cultures and periods—dark figures, a crushing weight, or an overwhelming sense of dread. Neuroscientists suggest that these recurring motifs stem from shared evolutionary fears, such as the need to remain vigilant against predators. In moments of perceived vulnerability, the brain's primal defense mechanisms may activate, creating hallucinations designed to heighten awareness and readiness to respond to threats, even if those threats are illusory.

The phenomenon also underscores the brain's incredible capacity for constructing reality. During sleep paralysis, the brain essentially creates a waking dream, blending the vividness of REM sleep with the self-awareness of wakefulness. This hybrid state challenges our understanding of perception and consciousness, revealing how the brain can convincingly fabricate entire sensory experiences in the absence of external input.

Despite the fear they evoke, these hallucinations are a testament to the brain's intricate and interconnected systems. They demonstrate the power of the mind to weave together emotions, memories, and sensory data into coherent, albeit often terrifying, narratives. Understanding the neuroscience of sleep paralysis not only helps demystify these experiences but also sheds light on the fragile boundary between wakefulness and sleep, a realm where reality and illusion collide spectacularly.

The Wake-Sleep Tug-of-War

The brainstem, particularly the *pons* and *medulla*, plays a pivotal role in regulating REM sleep. These regions are responsible for inducing muscle atonia while allowing the brain to remain active during dreaming. In sleep paralysis, the brainstem fails to release its hold on muscle atonia, even as the cerebral cortex—the part of the brain responsible for conscious thought—becomes alert. This mismatch creates the sensation of being awake but immobilized.

The Hallucination Factor

Hallucinations during sleep paralysis are thought to arise from the activation of the amygdala, a part of the brain associated with fear and emotional responses. The heightened activity in the amygdala during REM sleep can spill over into wakefulness, projecting vivid and often frightening imagery onto the real world.

The Brain's Interpretation of Fear

One of the most fascinating aspects of sleep paralysis is its ability to evoke primal fears. These fears are often universal—shadowy figures, suffocation, and feelings of malevolence—and they reflect the brain's instinctual responses to perceived threats.

Evolutionary Roots

From an evolutionary perspective, sleep paralysis may tap into survival instincts. The feeling of an "intruder" or a weight pressing on the chest could be remnants of ancient defense mechanisms, where hyper-vigilance to potential predators was essential.

Dr. Michael Cheyne, a psychologist specializing in sleep paralysis, posits, "The brain, caught in a liminal state between sleep and wakefulness, draws on its repository of fears to make sense of the physiological sensations it's experiencing. These fears are deeply ingrained in our evolutionary past."

The Neurochemical Orchestra

The transition between sleep and wakefulness is orchestrated by a complex interplay of neurotransmitters—chemical messengers that regulate brain activity.

Gamma-Aminobutyric Acid (GABA)

GABA is the primary inhibitory neurotransmitter in the brain, responsible for inducing muscle atonia during REM sleep. When GABA activity persists after the brain has awakened, it prevents voluntary movement, leading to the paralysis experienced during episodes.

Acetylcholine

Acetylcholine plays a critical role in initiating and maintaining REM sleep. An imbalance in acetylcholine signaling can prolong REM atonia, increasing the likelihood of sleep paralysis.

Dopamine and Serotonin

Dopamine and serotonin, two vital neurotransmitters in the brain, play crucial roles in regulating mood, alertness, and the transitions between sleep stages. These chemical messengers are deeply intertwined with the brain's ability to maintain a harmonious sleep-wake cycle, orchestrating the delicate shifts between various phases of sleep, including the pivotal REM stage. When their levels are well-balanced, they facilitate a smooth progression through the sleep stages, ensuring that the body and mind are aligned during the journey from dreaming to wakefulness.

Dopamine is closely linked to the regulation of wakefulness and arousal. It acts as a signal for transitioning out of sleep, gradually preparing the brain to re-engage with the external world. However, if dopamine activity becomes dysregulated, it can prematurely activate the brain during REM sleep. This creates a scenario where the individual becomes conscious before the body has fully lifted its natural REM-induced paralysis, leading to the unsettling phenomenon of sleep paralysis.

Serotonin, on the other hand, plays a foundational role in sleep regulation, particularly in the onset of sleep and the modulation of non-REM stages. It contributes to the calming of the brain, setting the stage for restorative rest. However, serotonin also acts as a precursor to melatonin, the hormone that governs the body's internal clock. Disruptions in serotonin levels can destabilize the timing of REM sleep, making it more likely for mismatches to occur between consciousness and the body's immobilized state.

Together, these neurotransmitters function as the brain's internal communicators, fine-tuning the transitions that allow for fluid movement between different sleep phases. When their levels are disturbed—whether by stress, medication, mental health conditions, or irregular sleep patterns—the resulting imbalance can disrupt these transitions, increasing the likelihood of experiencing sleep paralysis. This interplay between dopamine, serotonin, and sleep underscores the complexity of the brain's mechanisms, revealing how even minor fluctuations can ripple through the system, manifesting in profound and sometimes unsettling ways.

Moreover, disturbances in these neurotransmitters can amplify the vivid hallucinations and emotional intensity often reported during sleep paralysis. Dopamine's involvement in reward pathways and heightened sensory perception can contribute to the vividness of dream-like imagery. In contrast, serotonin's influence on emotional processing may heighten feelings of fear or awe during an episode. These overlapping roles highlight how deeply integrated these neurotransmitters are in shaping not just the mechanics of sleep but also the subjective experience of phenomena like sleep paralysis. Understanding their influence offers valuable insights into the brain's remarkable, albeit sometimes perplexing, inner workings.

Mapping the Brain During Sleep Paralysis

Advances in neuroimaging have provided valuable insights into the brain activity associated with sleep paralysis. Functional MRI (fMRI) and electroencephalography (EEG) studies reveal the following:

- **Hyperactivity in the Visual Cortex**: This accounts for the vivid and detailed hallucinations reported by many individuals.

- **Increased Activity in the Amygdala**: Responsible for the intense fear and emotional distress during episodes.

- **Suppressed Motor Cortex Activity**: Reflecting the persistence of muscle atonia despite the brain being awake.

Case Study: A Neurological Perspective

Case studies offer a window into the deeply personal yet scientifically fascinating experiences of sleep paralysis. Jacob, a 29-year-old teacher, sought help after enduring recurrent and distressing episodes. During a sleep study, researchers discovered that his episodes coincided with prolonged REM atonia—a state where the body remains immobilized during REM sleep—and heightened activity in the brainstem and amygdala, regions linked to motor control and fear processing.

"When the doctor showed me the scans, it was like seeing a map of my fear," Jacob reflected. "Understanding that it was my brain misfiring—and not a supernatural attack—helped me take the first step toward managing it." Armed with this insight, Jacob adopted healthier sleep habits and started a low-dose antidepressant to regulate serotonin levels. Over several months, his episodes became less frequent, and his new understanding of the condition helped alleviate much of the terror he once felt.

Similarly, Alisha, a 35-year-old artist, had her life disrupted by vivid hallucinations of shadowy figures during sleep paralysis. Initially, she avoided sleep, fearing the terrifying visions that awaited her. A neurological evaluation revealed irregular transitions between her REM and waking states, likely exacerbated by chronic stress. With therapy focused on stress management and practicing mindfulness techniques during the episodes, Alisha learned to navigate her experiences with a new sense of agency. Over time, she even began incorporating her hallucinations into her artwork, transforming her fear into a source of creative inspiration.

Another case involves Victor, a 42-year-old paramedic, who had been experiencing episodes since his teenage years. Convinced for years that he was being haunted, Victor avoided discussing his experiences out of fear of ridicule. When his wife encouraged him to seek medical advice, a sleep study revealed that his irregular shift work was disrupting his circadian rhythm, increasing the likelihood of sleep paralysis. Adjusting his schedule, incorporating regular exercise, and using a weighted blanket for grounding sensations during sleep helped reduce the severity of his episodes. "I didn't realize how much control I could have," Victor admitted. "The knowledge alone has been empowering."

These stories illustrate how understanding the neurological underpinnings of sleep paralysis can transform terror into empowerment. By shedding light on the delicate interplay of the brain's systems and equipping individuals with strategies to manage the condition, science provides a path toward not only relief but also personal growth.

The Intersection of Science and Experience

The neurological study of sleep paralysis unveils the intricate and delicate balance within the human brain, showcasing both its astonishing complexity and its moments of vulnerability. This exploration into the science behind sleep paralysis does not strip away its mystery; rather, it enhances the wonder of the experience. For those who endure it, the realization that their brain alone orchestrates such vivid and surreal hallucinations often deepens their fascination. It is a testament to the mind's power, capable of constructing entire worlds and emotions in the liminal space between wakefulness and sleep. Understanding the mechanisms—while grounding the experience in science—can also evoke awe for the profound connection between biology and perception, reminding us how little we truly know about the depths of consciousness.

Beyond the Science

Exploring sleep paralysis from a scientific perspective reveals much about the brain's intricate workings, but it also leaves us grappling with deeper, more profound questions. What is the true nature of consciousness? Why does fear, so primal and visceral, take center stage in these moments? And where exactly, lies the boundary between dreams and reality? Sleep paralysis resides in this enigmatic intersection, where science meets mystery, inviting us to peer beyond the mechanisms into the essence of human experience.

This phenomenon challenges the idea that consciousness is neatly confined to wakefulness or sleep, instead presenting it as fluid and multifaceted. During sleep paralysis, the waking mind is immersed in a dreamlike reality, blending the external world with vividly surreal hallucinations. This blending pushes us to reconsider our understanding of what is "real," forcing a confrontation with the malleability of perception and the ways the brain shapes our experience of the world.

At its core, sleep paralysis is more than a neurological glitch—it is a deeply personal journey that raises questions about fear's hold over the human mind. The intense dread often felt during these episodes seems to arise not solely from external stimuli but from within as if the subconscious mind magnifies hidden anxieties into tangible visions. This interplay between inner fears and external perception reveals the profound psychological landscape that sleep paralysis can illuminate.

Beyond its scientific explanations, sleep paralysis invites us to explore larger philosophical and spiritual ideas. Is it merely a product of the brain's misfiring, or does it touch something deeper, hinting at a connection to other realms of existence? For many, the vividness and emotional weight of these experiences suggest that they carry meaning beyond their biological roots, urging us to reflect on the limits of our understanding and the mysteries that lie just beyond reach.

The Brain's Sleep-Wake Duality

The brain's ability to manage the transitions between sleep and wakefulness is one of its most intricate and fascinating functions. It operates as a master conductor, orchestrating various processes to ensure restorative sleep while maintaining the capacity to wake swiftly when needed.

This delicate interplay hinges on a dual system that regulates sleep stages and transitions between them, balancing the physical restoration of the body with the psychological processing of the mind. However, even this finely tuned system is not immune to occasional misfires, and one of the most vivid manifestations of this is sleep paralysis.

During normal sleep, the brain navigates between non-rapid eye movement (NREM) sleep and rapid eye movement (REM) sleep in a structured cycle. NREM sleep is characterized by slower brain activity and serves as the foundation for physical repair and memory consolidation. REM sleep, on the other hand, is a period of heightened brain activity akin to a waking state, where dreams are most vivid, and the body undergoes atonia—a temporary paralysis preventing physical reactions to the dream world. This intricate choreography is managed by key brain regions, including the brainstem, which inhibits muscle movement during REM, and the thalamus, which filters sensory input to prevent external stimuli from interrupting sleep.

However, the very complexity that allows for these precise transitions also makes the system vulnerable to disruptions. Sleep paralysis occurs when there is a misalignment between the brain's wake systems and the mechanisms that maintain atonia during REM sleep. In these moments, a person becomes conscious while the body remains immobilized, trapped in a liminal state where the rules of sleep and wakefulness collide. This duality of the brain—designed to separate the dream world from reality—momentarily falters, creating a surreal and often unsettling experience.

What makes this phenomenon particularly fascinating is how it reveals the brain's layered architecture. In sleep paralysis, the waking brain attempts to make sense of the immobility and sensory distortions it encounters, often leading to vivid hallucinations. These sensory experiences are not random; they are shaped by the brain's natural processes. The hyperactivity of the amygdala, the brain's center for fear and threat detection, can imbue these episodes with an overwhelming sense of danger. Meanwhile, the cerebral cortex, responsible for higher-order thinking and perception, works overtime to rationalize the conflicting signals, sometimes generating images or scenarios that blend the surreal with the familiar.

This duality—the brain's role as both dream creator and reality interpreter—makes sleep paralysis a unique window into its capabilities and vulnerabilities. It underscores how the same mechanisms that allow for the restorative power of dreams can also give rise to some of the most vivid and intense experiences of human consciousness. Sleep paralysis is not merely a glitch; it is a testament to the complexity of the brain's sleep-wake system and its delicate balance between order and chaos. For those who experience it, these episodes can be both unsettling and awe-inspiring, a reminder of the mysterious interplay between the physical and the psychological realms within the human mind.

The Locus Coeruleus: Guardian of Arousal

The locus coeruleus, a tiny yet immensely powerful structure nestled within the brainstem, plays a pivotal role in the regulation of arousal, sleep, and the fine-tuned transitions between them. Often referred to as the brain's "guardian of arousal," this structure ensures that the boundaries between waking and dreaming remain intact. It operates like a vigilant gatekeeper, releasing norepinephrine, a neurotransmitter essential for alertness and focus, to shift the brain out of the dream world and into wakefulness. Simultaneously, it ensures that REM-related atonia—the paralysis that prevents the body from acting out dreams—remains confined to sleep.

However, this system, as precise as it is, is not immune to errors. During episodes of sleep paralysis, the locus coeruleus falters in its timing, creating a collision between REM-related atonia and waking consciousness. The individual awakens mentally but remains physically immobilized, trapped in a state where the body's motor systems are still under the inhibitory grip of REM sleep. This malfunction transforms the locus coeruleus from a seamless gatekeeper to an inadvertent jailor, locking the individual in a surreal and often terrifying experience.

Recent research has illuminated the critical role of norepinephrine irregularities in this process. Normally, the release of norepinephrine from the locus coeruleus helps transition the brain smoothly from sleep to wakefulness. In sleep paralysis, this release is disrupted, either delayed or insufficient, prolonging the paralysis and leaving the individual caught between states. This biochemical glitch doesn't just immobilize the body—it also amplifies the mind's response to the situation.

The delay in norepinephrine signaling has a cascading effect, activating the brain's fear circuitry, particularly the amygdala, which responds to the immobilization as if it were a direct threat. This hyperactivation creates an overwhelming sense of dread, even when no real danger exists. At the same time, the brain's sensory systems attempt to interpret the mismatch between wakefulness and atonia, often leading to vivid hallucinations or distorted perceptions. Shadowy figures, pressure on the chest, or strange sounds are the brain's attempt to rationalize the surreal experience, shaped by the heightened activity of the fear and arousal networks.

What makes the locus coeruleus so fascinating is its dual nature: it is both a protector of restful REM sleep and a critical player in awakening the mind. Its malfunction during sleep paralysis highlights the delicate balance required to maintain the boundaries between these states. When that balance is disrupted, the brain's natural systems of protection—such as atonia—become sources of fear and confusion.

Understanding the locus coeruleus role not only demystifies sleep paralysis but also underscores the extraordinary precision of the brain's sleep-wake systems. This small cluster of neurons, scarcely larger than a grain of rice, governs transitions that define our daily rhythms and ensure our safety during sleep. When its mechanisms falter, they reveal the fragility of these transitions and the profound interplay of neurochemistry, perception, and emotion. For those who have experienced sleep paralysis, the locus coeruleus stands as a reminder of both the power and the complexity of the human brain.

The Thalamus: A Signal Interpreter Gone Awry

The *thalamus* acts as a relay station, processing sensory information during wakefulness and filtering it during sleep. During sleep paralysis, the thalamus appears to oscillate between these two modes, causing the brain to interpret dream imagery as real-world stimuli. This misinterpretation is responsible for the sense of external threats—a shadowy figure in the room or a suffocating presence pressing down on the chest.

Fear, Memory, and the Amygdala

Fear is a defining characteristic of sleep paralysis. This fear isn't merely a reaction to the inability to move; it is amplified by the brain's memory and emotional centers.

Amygdala Overdrive

The *amygdala* becomes hyperactive during REM sleep, a state that carries over into sleep paralysis. Its role in detecting danger primes it to interpret neutral stimuli as life-threatening. For instance, a harmless shadow or a shift in lighting during an episode may trigger vivid hallucinations of malevolent beings.

Trauma's Role in Amplifying Sleep Paralysis

Trauma can further exacerbate the amygdala's response during sleep paralysis. Individuals with post-traumatic stress disorder (PTSD) often report heightened and recurring episodes, as their brains are already wired to remain on high alert. The overlap between trauma-related hypervigilance and sleep paralysis creates a perfect storm of heightened fear and distress.

The Sensory Illusions of Sleep Paralysis

During sleep paralysis, the brain engages in a phenomenon known as *multisensory integration failure*. This process involves the blending—or misblending—of sensory inputs, leading to the eerie realism of hallucinations.

The Body Schema Disruption

The brain maintains a constant map of the body, known as the *body schema*. In sleep paralysis, this map becomes disrupted, causing individuals to feel as though they are floating, being dragged, or pressed down. This sensation is often described as an out-of-body experience but is, in fact, the brain's struggle to reconcile sensory inputs with immobilized physical reality.

Auditory Hallucinations

One lesser-discussed aspect of sleep paralysis is the prevalence of auditory hallucinations. Many individuals report hearing footsteps, whispers, or even incomprehensible language during episodes. These auditory phenomena are thought to originate from overactivity in the auditory cortex combined with heightened fear responses, making innocuous background noise seem ominous and intentional.

The Brain's Plasticity in Sleep Paralysis

One of the most intriguing discoveries about sleep paralysis is its relationship with neuroplasticity—the brain's ability to adapt and rewire itself.

Habitual Sleep Paralysis

For individuals who experience frequent episodes, the brain may develop specific patterns of activation that make sleep paralysis more likely. This phenomenon is akin to a "learned" neural response, where the brain becomes conditioned to repeat the same missteps during transitions between sleep and wakefulness.

Recovery and Adaptation

Conversely, neuroplasticity also offers a path to recovery. Cognitive behavioral interventions, mindfulness practices, and even targeted sleep routines can help the brain rewire these maladaptive patterns, reducing the frequency and intensity of episodes.

Sleep Paralysis as a Window into Consciousness

Beyond its clinical implications, sleep paralysis offers profound insights into the nature of consciousness itself.

The Default Mode Network (DMN)

The *default mode network* (DMN), a set of interconnected brain regions active during rest and introspection, plays a key role during sleep paralysis. Research suggests that the DMN's activity during this state may contribute to the surreal blending of dreams and reality. This finding has implications for understanding how the brain constructs subjective experiences and navigates altered states of consciousness.

Lucid Dreaming and Sleep Paralysis

Interestingly, sleep paralysis shares neurological overlaps with lucid dreaming—a state where individuals become aware that they are dreaming and can sometimes exert control over their dreams. Both phenomena involve heightened activity in the prefrontal cortex, the region responsible for self-awareness and decision-making.

Some researchers propose that mastering lucid dreaming techniques could provide individuals with tools to cope with or even redirect sleep paralysis episodes, transforming them into less distressing or even empowering experiences.

Cutting-Edge Research

Modern neuroscience continues to unravel the mysteries of sleep paralysis, exploring its links to other phenomena such as:

- **Hypnagogic and Hypnopompic States**: The transitional moments between wakefulness and sleep, where sensory inputs and dream imagery overlap.
- **Temporal Lobe Epilepsy**: Some researchers hypothesize that subtle temporal lobe activity during sleep paralysis might account for its hallucinatory intensity.

- **Artificial Intelligence in Sleep Science**: AI-powered sleep studies are beginning to identify patterns in brain activity that could predict and prevent sleep paralysis, offering hope for targeted interventions.

Reflections on the Brain's Complexity

The brain's ability to weave dreams, fears, and reality into a seamless narrative is both a marvel and a mystery. Sleep paralysis, as unsettling as it may be, underscores the incredible complexity of the human mind—a system so advanced that even its glitches can produce profound and deeply meaningful experiences.

In the next chapter, we'll explore practical strategies for managing and mitigating sleep paralysis, combining scientific insights with actionable steps. For now, we leave this chapter with a deeper appreciation of the neurological wonders—and occasional missteps—that define our experience of consciousness.

Chapter 10:
The Psychology of Sleep Paralysis

The neurological basis of sleep paralysis paints a vivid picture of brain misfires and biological mechanisms, but it is only part of the story. The human mind—shaped by personal experiences, cultural beliefs, and subconscious fears—plays an equally significant role in shaping how sleep paralysis manifests and how individuals interpret these episodes.

This chapter delves into the psychological dimensions of sleep paralysis, examining how the mind influences the content, frequency, and intensity of episodes. From the role of stress and trauma to the impact of cultural narratives, we explore the interplay between psychology and this fascinating phenomenon.

The Role of Stress and Emotional States

Stress is a well-documented trigger for sleep paralysis, acting as a destabilizing force on the body's sleep-wake cycle.

Chronic Stress and Hypervigilance

When the brain is in a prolonged state of stress, the sympathetic nervous system remains hyperactive, priming the body for fight-or-flight responses. This heightened state of alertness increases the likelihood of sleep disruptions, including sleep paralysis.

For instance, individuals going through periods of significant life change—such as job loss, grief, or trauma—report higher instances of sleep paralysis. Their brains, already on high alert, struggle to transition smoothly between sleep stages.

Case Study: Stress-Induced Paralysis

Maria, a 34-year-old nurse, began experiencing sleep paralysis during the height of the COVID-19 pandemic. Working long hours under intense pressure, her sleep became fragmented, and she frequently woke during REM atonia. Her episodes often involved vivid hallucinations of patients calling her name or shadowy figures hovering over her bed.

Through therapy, Maria learned to recognize how her stress levels and sleep habits contributed to her experiences. Techniques such as mindfulness and structured sleep routines helped reduce her episodes and allowed her to regain a sense of control.

Trauma and It's Lingering Shadows

The psychological scars of trauma can deeply influence sleep paralysis, amplifying its severity and emotional impact.

Post-Traumatic Stress Disorder (PTSD)

For individuals with PTSD, the brain's fear response system is overactive, making them more susceptible to sleep disorders, including sleep paralysis. Episodes are often marked by recurring themes linked to the original trauma. For example, a survivor of an assault may experience hallucinations of being restrained or attacked during sleep paralysis.

Emotional Memory Encoding

The amygdala and hippocampus—key players in processing and storing emotional memories—become particularly active during REM sleep. Sleep paralysis episodes often draw upon these emotional memories, embedding them into hallucinations and creating vivid, personalized nightmares.

Cognitive Patterns and Interpretations

The way individuals interpret sleep paralysis can significantly shape their experience. Cognitive

distortions—irrational or exaggerated thought patterns—
often intensify the fear and helplessness associated with
episodes.

Catastrophic Thinking

Many individuals with sleep paralysis engage in
catastrophic thinking, believing they are dying, being
attacked, or experiencing a supernatural event. These
interpretations heighten the emotional response, making
episodes more terrifying and memorable.

Cognitive Behavioral Therapy (CBT)

CBT techniques have proven effective in reframing these
thought patterns. By challenging irrational beliefs and
replacing them with rational explanations, individuals can
reduce the emotional intensity of their episodes.

The Influence of Cultural Beliefs

Cultural narratives and societal beliefs play a powerful role
in shaping the content and interpretation of sleep
paralysis.

Supernatural Explanations

In many cultures, sleep paralysis is attributed to supernatural forces such as spirits, demons, or witches. These beliefs often create a self-reinforcing cycle: individuals who expect supernatural encounters are more likely to perceive their hallucinations as such.

- In Japan, sleep paralysis is called *kanashibari* and is believed to involve spirits binding the sleeper.
- In African cultures, episodes are often linked to witchcraft or ancestral intervention.
- In the United States, alien abduction narratives have become a common explanation for sleep paralysis experiences.

The Power of Expectation

Cultural beliefs not only influence how sleep paralysis is interpreted but can also shape the hallucinations themselves. Studies have found that individuals who are exposed to specific narratives—such as alien abductions—are more likely to incorporate those themes into their sleep paralysis episodes.

Psychological Coping Mechanisms

Understanding the psychological underpinnings of sleep paralysis can help individuals develop effective coping mechanisms.

Grounding Techniques

Grounding techniques involve focusing on physical sensations or environmental details to anchor oneself in reality. For example, some individuals use slow, deliberate breathing to calm their fear response and reduce the intensity of their hallucinations.

Imagery Rescripting

Imagery rescripting is a therapeutic technique in which individuals consciously reshape the content of their hallucinations. For example, a threatening shadow figure might be reimagined as a harmless visitor or even a source of comfort. This approach helps reduce the fear associated with sleep paralysis and empowers individuals to take control of their experiences.

Case Study: Resilience Through Awareness

Liam, a 22-year-old college student, began experiencing sleep paralysis after struggling with academic pressure and loneliness. His episodes often involved a recurring figure—a faceless man standing at the foot of his bed.

Through counseling, Liam explored how his feelings of isolation and anxiety were manifesting in his hallucinations. By addressing the underlying emotional issues and practicing imagery rescripting, he transformed the faceless figure into a representation of his inner strength. Over time, his episodes became less frequent and less distressing.

The Mind's Resilience

Sleep paralysis demonstrates the intricate interplay between the brain's physiological processes and the mind's psychological landscape. While its neurological roots are undeniable, the content and emotional impact of sleep paralysis is profoundly shaped by individual psychology.

Understanding this duality offers not only a deeper appreciation of the phenomenon but also a path toward empowerment and healing. By addressing the psychological factors that contribute to sleep paralysis, individuals can break free from their grip and reclaim their sense of safety in sleep.

In the next chapter, we will explore practical tools and therapeutic interventions that leverage these insights, offering actionable solutions to manage and prevent sleep paralysis. For now, we reflect on the mind's capacity to navigate even its most unsettling moments, transforming fear into understanding and resilience.

This chapter delves into the psychological aspects of sleep paralysis, weaving together stress, trauma, cultural narratives, and coping strategies to provide a richer understanding of the mind's role in shaping this phenomenon.

Chapter 11:
The Physiological Landscape of Sleep Paralysis

Sleep paralysis is not merely a product of the brain; it is a full-body experience that involves intricate interactions between the central nervous system, the autonomic nervous system, and the body's physiology. While the mind grapples with fear and hallucinations, the body remains inert, locked in a state of atonia. This chapter explores the physiological mechanisms that contribute to sleep paralysis, focusing on how the body's systems interact during these episodes and what physiological triggers may predispose individuals to this condition.

Atonia: The Body's Protective Mechanism

At the heart of sleep paralysis lies *atonia*, the temporary paralysis of voluntary muscles during REM sleep. Atonia serves as a protective function, preventing the sleeper from physically acting out their dreams. However, during sleep paralysis, this paralysis persists even as the mind regains wakefulness, creating a profound disconnect between intent and action.

The Role of Spinal Motor Neurons

During REM sleep, the brain sends inhibitory signals to the spinal motor neurons via the medulla and pons. These signals suppress muscle activity, effectively "cutting off" voluntary movement.

In sleep paralysis, this inhibition remains intact even when higher brain functions, such as consciousness, are reactivated. This disconnect creates the sensation of being trapped within one's body, unable to move or cry out.

Peripheral Nervous System Involvement

Interestingly, the peripheral nervous system (PNS) also plays a role in sleep paralysis. The PNS governs involuntary bodily functions, such as breathing and heartbeat, and these functions often become a focal point during episodes. Many individuals report sensations of restricted breathing or a heavy weight on the chest, which may stem from the PNS's regulation of diaphragm and intercostal muscle activity during REM atonia.

The Autonomic Nervous System's Paradox

The autonomic nervous system (ANS), which controls involuntary processes like heart rate and respiration, behaves paradoxically during sleep paralysis.

Sympathetic Overdrive

Sleep paralysis often triggers a surge of activity in the sympathetic nervous system (SNS), the branch of the ANS responsible for the fight-or-flight response. This overactivation occurs because the brain perceives the inability to move as a threat, even though the body is technically safe.

Symptoms such as increased heart rate, sweating, and a sense of impending doom are hallmarks of this sympathetic overdrive. The heightened physiological arousal feeds into the emotional fear, creating a feedback loop that amplifies the distress.

Respiratory Perception

The sensation of suffocation reported during sleep paralysis is another function of the ANS. While breathing is not actually impaired, the brain's heightened state of awareness can exaggerate the perception of restricted airflow. This is compounded by the fact that REM-related atonia limits the activity of the accessory muscles involved in deep breathing, making respiration feel shallow.

Hormonal Interactions

Hormones play a crucial role in regulating sleep cycles and physiological responses during sleep paralysis.

Cortisol: The Stress Hormone

Cortisol, a hormone released in response to stress, may contribute to the development of sleep paralysis. High cortisol levels, often associated with chronic stress or sleep deprivation, disrupt the body's natural sleep architecture. This disruption increases the likelihood of awakening during REM sleep, creating the conditions for sleep paralysis.

Melatonin and Circadian Rhythms

Melatonin, the hormone responsible for regulating the sleep-wake cycle, may also influence sleep paralysis. Irregular melatonin production—often caused by erratic sleep schedules or exposure to artificial light—can destabilize the transitions between sleep stages, making episodes more likely.

The Physiological Sensations of Sleep Paralysis

One of the most unsettling aspects of sleep paralysis is the intensity and realism of the physical sensations experienced during episodes. These sensations are not hallucinations but rather misinterpretations or amplifications of real physiological processes.

Chest Pressure

The sensation of a weight on the chest, often described as a supernatural presence, is linked to the brain's interpretation of normal respiratory effort during atonia. The body's inability to engage accessory breathing muscles creates a sense of restriction, which the mind may anthropomorphize into a figure or force.

Vibrations and Tingling

Many individuals report sensations of vibrations or tingling throughout their bodies during sleep paralysis. These phenomena are thought to arise from heightened sensory awareness as the brain transitions between REM and wakefulness, coupled with the nervous system's partial activation.

Temperature Fluctuations

Episodes of sleep paralysis are often accompanied by feelings of intense heat or cold. These sensations may result from the autonomic nervous system's fluctuating activity as the sympathetic and parasympathetic branches attempt to regain equilibrium.

Predisposing Physiological Factors

Certain physiological factors increase an individual's susceptibility to sleep paralysis.

Sleep Deprivation

One of the most significant contributors is sleep deprivation. A lack of restorative sleep disrupts the body's natural cycles, making transitions between sleep stages more erratic.

Irregular Sleep Schedules

Shift workers and individuals with jet lag often experience higher rates of sleep paralysis. Irregular schedules disrupt the circadian rhythm, leading to misaligned sleep-wake transitions.

Comorbid Sleep Disorders

Conditions such as sleep apnea and narcolepsy are strongly associated with sleep paralysis. Sleep apnea, which causes interruptions in breathing during sleep, can fragment REM cycles, while narcolepsy directly impacts the regulation of REM sleep.

Case Study: The Physiology of Paralysis

Ethan, a 45-year-old software engineer, began experiencing sleep paralysis after taking on a demanding project that required him to work late nights. He described episodes where he felt as though he was being crushed by an invisible force.

A sleep study revealed that Ethan's episodes coincided with fragmented REM cycles and shallow breathing patterns. With the help of a sleep specialist, Ethan implemented a consistent sleep schedule and began using relaxation techniques to regulate his autonomic responses. Over time, his episodes became less frequent and less severe.

Understanding the Body's Role

While the brain's role in sleep paralysis is well-documented, the body's physiological contributions offer a vital piece of the puzzle. The interplay between muscle atonia, autonomic arousal, and hormonal regulation underscores the complexity of this condition.

Recognizing the body's involvement not only deepens our understanding of sleep paralysis but also highlights new avenues for managing and preventing episodes. Techniques that address physiological triggers—such as breathing exercises, stress reduction, and sleep hygiene—can provide significant relief.

In the next chapter, we'll explore the historical and cultural evolution of sleep paralysis, tracing its depictions across time and geography to uncover how societies have made sense of this mysterious condition. For now, we marvel at the intricate choreography of the body and mind, a dance that occasionally falters but ultimately speaks to the profound complexity of human physiology.

The next chapter dives deeply into the physiological mechanisms of sleep paralysis, providing a fresh perspective on its bodily dimensions.

Chapter 12:

Sleep Paralysis Across Time and Cultures

Sleep paralysis is not a modern phenomenon; it has existed for centuries, deeply woven into the fabric of human history. Its occurrence has been chronicled in folklore, religion, art, and literature across diverse cultures. These interpretations reflect humanity's attempts to understand and contextualize an experience that is both universal and deeply personal.

This chapter explores the historical and cultural dimensions of sleep paralysis, offering a deeper look at how it has been perceived, explained, and mythologized. From ancient legends to contemporary narratives, we trace the evolution of our understanding and how these cultural frameworks shape the experience itself.

Ancient Origins: Mythology and the Supernatural

Before the advent of scientific inquiry, sleep paralysis was often attributed to supernatural forces. Ancient societies interpreted the condition through the lens of their spiritual and mythological beliefs.

The "Old Hag" and European Folklore

In medieval Europe, sleep paralysis was frequently associated with witchcraft or demonic possession. One of the most enduring legends is that of the "Old Hag," a witch-like figure who was believed to sit on the chest of the sleeper, suffocating them.

This imagery not only captured the sensation of chest pressure but also reflected societal anxieties about witches and malevolent spirits. The term "hag-ridden" even entered the vernacular, signifying someone tormented by supernatural forces during sleep.

Ancient Greece and Rome

In ancient Greece, sleep paralysis was sometimes linked to visits from gods or spirits. Hypnos (the god of sleep) and Thanatos (the personification of death) were thought to hover between the worlds of the living and the dead, influencing the dream states of mortals. Romans attributed the condition to incubus and succubus demons, believed to sexually assault sleeping individuals.

Cross-Cultural Narratives

Sleep paralysis experiences are remarkably similar worldwide, but the interpretations vary dramatically depending on cultural context.

East Asia: Kanashibari and Ghostly Bonds

In Japan, sleep paralysis is known as *kanashibari*, a term that originally referred to the magical binding of a person's body by monks or spirits. Japanese accounts often describe shadowy figures or vengeful spirits immobilizing the sleeper, reflecting the cultural significance of ancestral spirits and ghosts.

In China, similar experiences are referred to as *gui ya chuang,* meaning "ghost pressing on the body." The belief that malevolent spirits cause sleep paralysis is deeply embedded in traditional Chinese folklore, often tied to improper burial practices or unresolved familial tensions.

The Middle East: Jinn Encounters

In Islamic cultures, sleep paralysis is often attributed to encounters with jinn—supernatural beings mentioned in the Quran. Jinn is believed to inhabit a parallel world and occasionally interact with humans, causing unexplained phenomena. Sleep paralysis episodes involving shadowy or whispering entities are often interpreted as jinn attempting to control or harm the sleeper.

African and Afro-Caribbean Traditions

In many African cultures, sleep paralysis is linked to witchcraft or ancestral intervention. Among Afro-

Caribbean communities, such as those practicing Vodou, episodes are often interpreted as spiritual possessions or curses. These interpretations reinforce the role of spiritual rituals and protections in managing such experiences.

Artistic and Literary Depictions

Sleep paralysis has long inspired artists and writers, serving as both a subject and a metaphor for fear, vulnerability, and the unknown.

Fuseli's The Nightmare

One of the most famous artistic representations of sleep paralysis is Henry Fuseli's painting *The Nightmare* (1781). The painting depicts a woman in a state of distress, a demonic figure perched on her chest, and a spectral horse looming in the background. Fuseli's work vividly captures the dread and surreal imagery associated with sleep paralysis, cementing its place in the Western cultural imagination.

Gothic Literature

In the Gothic literature of the 18th and 19th centuries, sleep paralysis was often intertwined with themes of the supernatural. Writers such as Edgar Allan Poe and Mary Shelley drew upon the condition to evoke feelings of terror and helplessness, using it as a narrative device to blur the line between reality and the surreal.

Modern Narratives: Alien Abductions and Sci-Fi

n contemporary Western culture, sleep paralysis has found a compelling new narrative home in the realm of science fiction, particularly in stories involving alien abductions, extraterrestrial encounters, and advanced technologies. These modern interpretations often reflect the evolving fears and fascinations of society, blending the unexplained sensations of sleep paralysis with themes of otherworldly contact and technological intrusion. The experiences of those who have sleep paralysis—immobility, vivid hallucinations, and a sense of a presence in the room—align closely with the imagery of alien abductions popularized in media, leading some individuals to interpret their episodes as evidence of extraterrestrial phenomena.

The cultural phenomenon of alien abduction narratives became prominent in the mid-20th century, coinciding with the space race, the dawn of the nuclear age, and increasing societal awareness of the possibility of life beyond Earth. During this time, reports of alien encounters often shared eerily similar details: individuals described waking up paralyzed, unable to move or speak, while shadowy figures or humanoid beings hovered nearby. These beings, commonly referred to as "greys," were often depicted as slender, hairless, and with large, black, almond-shaped eyes. Witnesses reported sensations of being observed, touched, or even transported to unfamiliar environments, such as spacecraft or surreal alien landscapes.

Many of these accounts mirror the common symptoms of sleep paralysis, including **a sense of presence**, **chest pressure**, and **hallucinatory visuals**. The inability to move, coupled with the vivid imagery of shadowy figures, has made sleep paralysis fertile ground for alien abduction stories. For individuals experiencing these episodes, the vividness of the hallucinations—often heightened by the brain's partial wakefulness—makes the events feel intensely real, leaving a lasting psychological impact.

Popular Media and Sleep Paralysis in Sci-Fi

The relationship between sleep paralysis and alien abduction narratives has been further amplified by popular culture. Science fiction books, television series, and films have borrowed heavily from these experiences to craft stories that blur the line between horror, mystery, and wonder. Shows like *The X-Files* and films such as *Close Encounters of the Third Kind* and *Communion* popularized the archetype of abductions during sleep, where characters are immobilized and subjected to examinations or probing by extraterrestrial beings. These works not only entertain audiences but also reflect humanity's deeper fears surrounding vulnerability, invasion, and the unknown.

Author Whitley Strieber's book *Communion* (1987) became one of the most notable examples linking alien abductions with the experiences of sleep paralysis. Strieber recounted his terrifying encounters with extraterrestrial beings, which often occurred during the night while he lay in bed paralyzed. The detailed and vivid descriptions of his experiences resonated with readers, many of whom reported similar episodes of immobility, hallucinations, and overwhelming fear. While Strieber framed his experiences through the lens of alien contact, scientists have suggested that his accounts align closely with sleep paralysis phenomena.

Similarly, movies like *The Fourth Kind* (2009) capitalize on the overlap between sleep paralysis and alien abduction reports. Set in Alaska, the film dramatizes disturbing abduction cases where victims experience being paralyzed in their beds, often witnessing shadowy figures and feeling as though they were forcibly taken from their homes. By linking sleep disturbances with alien encounters, the film mirrors the very real sensations of helplessness and fear reported by those with sleep paralysis.

Psychological Interpretations

From a psychological perspective, alien abduction narratives may represent the brain's attempt to rationalize the disturbing and unfamiliar sensations of sleep paralysis. The brain seeks explanations for the hallucinatory imagery and physical sensations that accompany the condition. In contemporary Western culture—where aliens have become a prominent trope—extraterrestrial encounters provide a culturally relevant framework for interpreting these surreal experiences. For individuals living in a society fascinated by space exploration and technological advancement, the idea of being abducted by intelligent beings aligns with both modern anxieties and collective imaginations.

The **"sense of presence"**—a hallmark of sleep paralysis—plays a particularly significant role in alien abduction narratives. Neuroscientific studies have linked this phenomenon to activity in the brain's temporoparietal junction (TPJ), an area responsible for integrating sensory information about the body and its environment. When this region is disrupted, as it often is during sleep paralysis, individuals may experience a distorted sense of self and the perception of another being nearby. The brain fills in the sensory gaps, sometimes projecting images of alien figures or other entities that align with cultural expectations.

The Role of Technology and the Future

The modern era's fixation on technology and advanced intelligence has further shaped the alien abduction narrative. Sleep paralysis experiences are increasingly interpreted through a technological lens, with individuals reporting sensations of being monitored, examined, or manipulated by advanced machines or robotic beings. This reflects broader societal concerns about surveillance, loss of privacy, and humanity's increasing dependence on technology. As artificial intelligence, drones, and virtual reality become more prevalent, these themes may continue to shape the way people interpret their experiences of sleep paralysis.

Some theorists and cultural critics argue that alien abduction stories serve as modern myths, replacing older folklore about demons, spirits, and witches that were historically used to explain sleep paralysis. In medieval Europe, for instance, the condition was often attributed to the **"Old Hag"** or malevolent spirits pressing down on the sleeper's chest. Today, in a more scientifically oriented and technologically driven society, these same experiences are reimagined through the framework of extraterrestrials and advanced beings.

Conclusion

The modern narratives surrounding alien abductions and science fiction provide a fascinating cultural lens through which to understand sleep paralysis. While the physiological roots of sleep paralysis lie in disruptions to the REM sleep cycle, the way individuals interpret their experiences is heavily influenced by cultural stories and societal beliefs. In contemporary Western culture, the prevalence of alien abduction imagery reflects humanity's evolving fears and curiosity about the unknown, whether it takes the form of life beyond Earth or technological advancements.

For those experiencing sleep paralysis, these narratives offer both explanation and validation. They transform unsettling episodes into stories of cosmic mystery, inviting individuals to view their experiences not just as random malfunctions of the brain but as encounters with something larger and stranger than themselves. Whether one interprets these moments as neurological quirks or glimpses into alternate realities, they remind us of the power of the human mind to create meaning from even the most inexplicable phenomena.

Alien Abduction Stories

The rise of alien abduction narratives in the 20th century coincided with increased interest in sleep disorders. Many purported abductees describe experiences that align closely with sleep paralysis, including immobilization, intrusive entities, and feelings of helplessness.

Neurologists have noted the similarities between these accounts and traditional folklore, suggesting that cultural influences shape the specific imagery of sleep paralysis episodes. Where one culture might see a ghost or demon, another sees extraterrestrial beings.

Sleep Paralysis and Cultural Identity

The cultural framing of sleep paralysis does more than provide explanations—it influences how individuals experience and interpret their episodes.

Cultural Shaping of Hallucinations

Studies have shown that cultural narratives can directly impact the content of sleep paralysis hallucinations. For instance, individuals raised in societies with strong supernatural beliefs are more likely to report ghostly or demonic figures. At the same time, those in secular or scientific environments may describe more abstract or psychological phenomena.

The Role of Rituals and Remedies

Cultural practices also play a role in addressing sleep paralysis. In communities where the condition is attributed to supernatural causes, rituals such as exorcisms, prayers, or protective charms are often employed. While these practices may not address the neurological basis of sleep paralysis, they can provide psychological relief and a sense of agency.

Revisiting History Through Modern Science

Historical and cultural narratives of sleep paralysis provide valuable insights into the human psyche and our need to explain the inexplicable. Modern science, while demystifying the condition, also highlights its universality.

Bridging the Gap

By acknowledging both scientific and cultural perspectives, we can develop a more holistic understanding of sleep paralysis. Recognizing its dual nature—both as a physiological event and a culturally shaped experience—enables us to appreciate the richness and diversity of human perception.

Reflections on the Human Experience

Sleep paralysis serves as a powerful reminder of the shared aspects of human experience across time and geography. Its consistent themes—immobility, fear, and the interplay between the seen and unseen—underscore the universality of our struggles with the unknown.

In the next chapter, we'll explore practical interventions and cutting-edge treatments that draw upon both scientific insights and cultural understanding to address sleep paralysis. For now, we reflect on the ways in which humanity has sought to make sense of this enigmatic state, weaving it into the fabric of our collective imagination.

Chapter 13:

Conquering the Shadows— Practical Interventions for Sleep Paralysis

While sleep paralysis may feel like an unyielding mystery, modern science and ancient wisdom offer numerous strategies to manage and mitigate its occurrence, addressing the condition requires a holistic approach that incorporates lifestyle changes, psychological techniques, and, in some cases, medical interventions.

This chapter dives deeply into the practical solutions available, providing readers with actionable tools to regain control and confidence in their sleep. From cultivating healthy sleep hygiene to exploring therapeutic approaches, this chapter empowers readers to move beyond fear and take proactive steps toward restful, paralysis-free nights.

Lifestyle Adjustments: The Foundation of Prevention

The first step in addressing sleep paralysis is to establish a solid foundation of healthy sleep habits. These adjustments can reduce the likelihood of fragmented sleep cycles and the disruptions that trigger episodes.

Sleep Hygiene

Good sleep hygiene is essential for maintaining a stable sleep-wake cycle. Key practices include:

- **Consistent Sleep Schedule**: Going to bed and waking up at the same time daily regulates the circadian rhythm.

- **Creating a Sleep-Inducing Environment**: A cool, dark, and quiet bedroom promotes deeper, more restorative sleep.
- **Limiting Stimulants**: Reducing caffeine and alcohol intake, especially in the evening, minimizes sleep disruptions.

Managing Stress and Anxiety

Stress is a major contributor to sleep paralysis. Stress reduction techniques such as mindfulness meditation, yoga, and breathing exercises can help calm the mind and body before sleep.

Case Study: Grounding Techniques for Stress Relief

Emma, a 29-year-old graduate student, frequently experienced sleep paralysis during exam periods. Her therapist introduced her to grounding techniques, such as focusing on the sensation of her feet touching the floor or counting her breaths. These simple practices helped Emma manage her anxiety, significantly reducing her episodes.

Targeting Sleep Stages: Enhancing REM Regulation

Sleep paralysis often arises during transitions between REM sleep and wakefulness. Strategies that improve REM sleep continuity can lower the risk of episodes.

Limiting Sleep Fragmentation

Interruptions in sleep, such as those caused by noise, restless leg syndrome, or sleep apnea, increase the likelihood of waking during REM. Using tools like white noise machines, weighted blankets, or CPAP devices for sleep apnea can improve overall sleep quality.

Tracking Sleep Patterns

Modern sleep-tracking devices provide valuable insights into one's sleep architecture, helping identify patterns that may predispose individuals to sleep paralysis. Apps and wearable devices that monitor sleep cycles can guide adjustments to sleep habits.

Cognitive and Psychological Techniques

The mind plays a critical role in the experience of sleep paralysis, and psychological interventions can help reshape how episodes are perceived and managed.

Cognitive Behavioral Therapy for Sleep Paralysis (CBT-SP)

CBT-SP focuses on reframing the negative thoughts and fears associated with sleep paralysis. By identifying and challenging catastrophic thinking patterns—such as the belief that episodes signify danger—CBT-SP helps reduce emotional distress and the frequency of episodes.

Imagery Rehearsal Therapy (IRT)

IRT allows individuals to reshape recurring themes in their hallucinations. For example, a threatening shadow figure can be mentally reimagined as a harmless presence. Practicing these new narratives in waking life can influence the brain's response during episodes, making them less frightening.

Example: Transforming Fearful Encounters Liam, a 40-year-old artist, used IRT to transform the dark figure that haunted his sleep paralysis into a glowing, protective light. Over time, this practice not only diminished his fear but also reduced the frequency of his episodes.

Cutting-Edge Medical Interventions

For individuals with chronic or severe sleep paralysis, medical interventions may be necessary.

Medication

Medications that regulate REM sleep or address underlying conditions such as anxiety and depression can be helpful. Common options include:

- **Antidepressants**: SSRIs or tricyclic antidepressants can suppress REM sleep, reducing episodes.
- **Melatonin Supplements**: These can help stabilize the sleep-wake cycle, particularly in individuals with irregular schedules.

Addressing Comorbid Conditions

Treating underlying sleep disorders, such as narcolepsy or insomnia, often reduces sleep paralysis. Collaboration with a sleep specialist can provide a comprehensive approach to diagnosis and treatment.

Alternative and Complementary Practices

Beyond conventional medicine, alternative approaches have shown promise in managing sleep paralysis.

Lucid Dreaming Techniques

Lucid dreaming—becoming aware of and controlling dreams—offers a unique approach to managing sleep paralysis. Training the mind to recognize dream states can empower individuals to take control during episodes, turning fear into curiosity.

Traditional Practices and Rituals

In cultures where sleep paralysis is attributed to spiritual forces, rituals and practices such as protective prayers, talismans, or herbal remedies provide comfort and reassurance. While these may not address the neurological basis of sleep paralysis, their psychological benefits can be profound.

Cultural Case Study: Protective Rituals In a small village in Nigeria, community members who experience sleep paralysis often seek guidance from elders. Rituals involving symbolic cleansing and protective charms not only alleviate fear but also reinforce a sense of community and support.

Empowering Through Knowledge

Education is a powerful tool in reducing the stigma and fear surrounding sleep paralysis. By understanding its physiological and psychological roots, individuals can shift their perspective from one of helplessness to empowerment.

Community Support

Support groups, both online and offline, provide spaces for individuals to share their experiences and strategies. Knowing they are not alone can significantly reduce the fear and isolation that often accompany sleep paralysis.

The Road to Restful Sleep

Sleep paralysis may never be completely eradicated for some, but it can be managed and transformed into a less distressing experience. Combining lifestyle changes, psychological techniques, and medical interventions offers a multifaceted approach that addresses the condition from all angles.

As we move to the next chapter, we will explore the intriguing connections between sleep paralysis and creativity, investigating how this condition has inspired art, innovation, and self-discovery. For now, the tools outlined in this chapter serve as a beacon of hope, guiding readers toward nights of peaceful, unbroken sleep.

This chapter provides actionable insights and practical interventions for managing sleep paralysis.

Chapter 14:

Sleep Paralysis and the Spark of Creativity

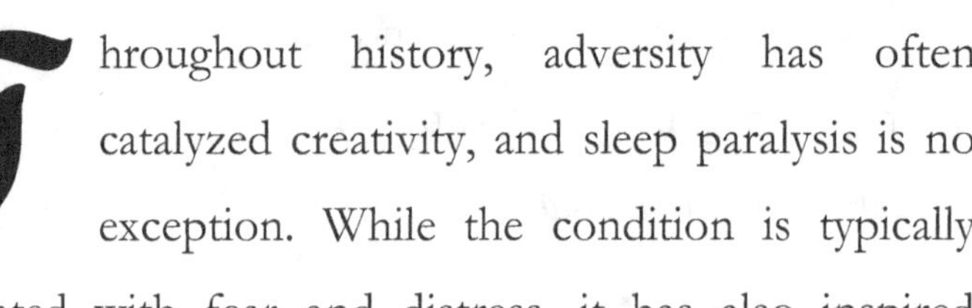

Throughout history, adversity has often catalyzed creativity, and sleep paralysis is no exception. While the condition is typically associated with fear and distress, it has also inspired profound works of art, literature, and innovation. For some, sleep paralysis offers a unique window into the workings of the subconscious mind, bridging the gap between the waking world and the dreamscape.

This chapter delves into the unexpected connection between sleep paralysis and creativity, exploring how the condition has influenced creative expression, enhanced problem-solving, and fostered deeper self-awareness.

The Dreamscape of Sleep Paralysis

Sleep paralysis resides in a liminal space where the boundaries between wakefulness and dreaming blur. This altered state of consciousness often produces vivid imagery and heightened emotions, resembling a waking dream. For artists, writers, and thinkers, such experiences can become a wellspring of inspiration.

Hypnagogic Hallucinations as Creative Fuel

The hallucinations experienced during sleep paralysis—ranging from shadowy figures to surreal landscapes—are strikingly vivid. These images can linger long after an episode ends, providing fertile ground for creative exploration.

Case Study: An Artist's Inspiration Sofia, a contemporary painter from Brazil, uses her sleep paralysis experiences as a central theme in her work. One recurring image—a figure dissolving into a cascade of light—became the centerpiece of her acclaimed exhibit, "In the

Grip of Shadows." For Sofia, the terrifying nature of sleep paralysis was transformed into a source of beauty and meaning.

Sleep Paralysis in Literature and Storytelling

Sleep paralysis has long been a source of fascination for writers, appearing in literary works that span centuries and genres.

Gothic Literature and the Supernatural

The haunting imagery of sleep paralysis aligns perfectly with the themes of Gothic literature. Writers such as Edgar Allan Poe and Mary Shelley drew upon the condition to evoke feelings of terror and the sublime. Poe's tales, in particular, often depict protagonists who experience paralysis or states of heightened awareness, blurring the lines between life and death.

Modern Science Fiction

In contemporary times, sleep paralysis has found a home in the realm of science fiction. Stories involving alien abductions, alternate dimensions, and advanced technologies often draw upon the universal experience of being immobilized while conscious. These narratives not only entertain but also reflect humanity's evolving understanding of the mind.

Creativity Through the Lens of Neuroscience

From a scientific perspective, the connection between sleep paralysis and creativity may stem from the brain's heightened activity during REM sleep.

Enhanced Connectivity

During REM sleep, the brain exhibits increased connectivity between regions responsible for emotion, memory, and imagination. Sleep paralysis, occurring at the threshold of REM and wakefulness, may allow individuals to consciously access these enhanced states.

Problem-Solving and Insight

The altered consciousness experienced during sleep paralysis can also foster novel ways of thinking. Many individuals report experiencing profound insights or revelations during episodes, often described as "eureka moments." This phenomenon aligns with research suggesting that REM sleep enhances creative problem-solving.

Example: Scientific Breakthroughs and Dreams While not directly related to sleep paralysis, famous examples such as Dmitri Mendeleev's dream-inspired creation of the periodic table illustrate how altered states of consciousness can spark innovation. Sleep paralysis, with its vivid and often surreal quality, offers similar opportunities for breakthroughs.

Artistic Expression as a Coping Mechanism

For individuals who experience frequent or distressing sleep paralysis, creative expression can serve as both an outlet and a form of therapy.

Transforming Fear into Art

Channeling the emotions and imagery of sleep paralysis into art, writing, or music allows individuals to externalize their experiences. This process can reduce fear and foster a sense of mastery over the condition.

Case Study: Music Inspired by Sleep Paralysis Alyssa, a composer from Canada, wrote a hauntingly beautiful symphony based on her sleep paralysis episodes. The piece, titled "Between Waking and Dreaming," incorporates dissonant chords and shifting rhythms to evoke the surreal and unsettling nature of the condition. For Alyssa, composing the symphony helped her reframe sleep paralysis as a source of inspiration rather than fear.

The Subconscious Mirror

Sleep paralysis often brings subconscious fears, desires, and unresolved emotions to the surface. For some, this can lead to a deeper understanding of themselves and their inner world.

Jungian Perspectives

Carl Jung, the famed psychoanalyst, viewed dreams and altered states as windows into the collective unconscious. Sleep paralysis, with its rich and often symbolic imagery, can be interpreted through a Jungian lens as a dialogue between the conscious and subconscious mind.

Example: The Shadow Archetype The shadowy figures commonly seen during sleep paralysis episodes can be understood as manifestations of the "shadow self"—the parts of the psyche that are repressed or hidden. Engaging with these images, rather than fearing them, can lead to profound personal growth.

Sleep Paralysis in Collective Creativity

Beyond individual experiences, sleep paralysis has influenced collective culture and shared narratives.

Shared Experiences in Folklore

As explored in earlier chapters, sleep paralysis has given rise to myths and legends that resonate across cultures. These shared stories not only provide a sense of community but also reflect the universal human quest to make meaning of the unknown.

The Role of Media

Modern media, including films and documentaries, continues to draw upon sleep paralysis as a source of inspiration. Works like the film *The Nightmare* (2015) bring the phenomenon to a wider audience, fostering both awareness and fascination.

Unlocking Creative Potential

For those willing to embrace the unknown, sleep paralysis can become a tool for unlocking creativity. Techniques such as dream journaling, mindfulness, and lucid dreaming can help individuals harness the imagery and insights of their episodes in constructive ways.

Reflections on the Creative Spirit

Sleep paralysis is often viewed solely as a source of fear, but it also holds the potential for transformation. By reframing these experiences as opportunities for self-expression and discovery, individuals can move beyond the shadows and into the light of creativity.

In the next chapter, we will explore the intersection of sleep paralysis and spirituality, examining how the condition has shaped beliefs about the soul, the afterlife, and the nature of existence. For now, we celebrate the resilience and creativity of the human spirit, capable of turning even the most unsettling experiences into sources of inspiration.

This chapter highlights the profound connection between sleep paralysis and creativity, offering insights into how this mysterious condition can inspire art, literature, and self-discovery.

Chapter 15:

Sleep Paralysis and Spirituality—A Gateway to the Beyond

Sleep paralysis has long held a unique place in the intersection of the physical and the metaphysical, often evoking a profound sense of mystery and wonder. This phenomenon, where consciousness is caught in a liminal space between wakefulness and dreaming, transcends mere biology and ventures into the realm of spirituality. Across cultures and epochs, sleep paralysis has been interpreted not as a mere quirk of the brain but as a doorway to realms unseen—a bridge between the material and the spiritual.

For centuries, individuals experiencing sleep paralysis have reported encounters that defy logical explanation. Shadowy figures, luminous beings, or even ancestral spirits often populate these vivid episodes. To those immersed in spiritual traditions, these experiences are far more than hallucinations; they are regarded as moments of heightened perception where the veil separating worlds becomes thin. The narratives of these encounters are striking in their depth and diversity, echoing ancient beliefs about the soul's journey, divine revelations, and connections to other dimensions.

Many spiritual practitioners view sleep paralysis as a rare opportunity to access altered states of consciousness. This state, where the body remains inert while the mind is active, is sometimes seen as an ideal gateway for astral projection—the deliberate exploration of spiritual realms beyond the physical body. Such practices are steeped in ancient wisdom, appearing in the mystical teachings of cultures as diverse as the Egyptians, Hindus, and indigenous shamans. For them, sleep paralysis represents a controlled threshold, a chance to transcend the ordinary and engage with the extraordinary.

The spiritual lens transforms sleep paralysis from a source of terror to a medium of connection and growth. Fear— a common response to these episodes—is often reframed as the ego's resistance to the unknown. By leaning into the experience rather than recoiling from it, individuals can discover profound insights about themselves and the universe. Meditation, prayer, and focused breathing are often employed during sleep paralysis to shift the experience from fear to curiosity, opening the door to potentially transformative encounters.

In spiritual traditions, such experiences are not random but deeply meaningful. The recurring themes of shadowy entities or radiant light figures can serve as metaphors for personal struggles, unresolved conflicts, or even spiritual guardianship. Encounters with these entities are frequently interpreted as messages or tests, pushing the experiencer to confront fears, embrace growth, or seek higher truths. The boundaries between the real and the symbolic blur turn sleep paralysis into a deeply personal spiritual odyssey.

The connection between sleep paralysis and spirituality is further enriched by shared stories and collective understanding. Across the world, communities have gathered to share their experiences, finding solace and meaning in the recognition of shared visions. These narratives have inspired countless myths, legends, and artistic expressions, embedding sleep paralysis deeply in the human cultural and spiritual tapestry. Whether seen as warnings, blessings, or mere glimpses into the divine, these shared accounts highlight the profound impact of such experiences on individuals and communities alike.

Yet, the spiritual interpretation of sleep paralysis is not without its challenges. The experience can be overwhelming, leaving individuals questioning the nature of reality itself. But herein lies its power: the discomfort forces introspection, inviting the experiencer to redefine their understanding of existence. Those who embrace the spiritual aspects of sleep paralysis often describe a heightened sense of purpose, connection, and enlightenment, transforming their fear into empowerment.

In navigating this enigmatic phenomenon, spirituality offers tools and perspectives that ground the extraordinary in meaning. Sleep paralysis, when viewed through this lens, becomes not a mere neurological glitch but a profound invitation to explore the mysteries of the universe and the depths of the self. It challenges us to expand our perceptions of reality, embrace the unknown, and find harmony in the interplay between the seen and unseen. For those willing to approach it with an open heart and mind, sleep paralysis can indeed serve as a gateway to the beyond—a journey that is as transformative as it is mysterious.

Sleep paralysis has long been associated with spiritual and metaphysical experiences. For centuries, people across cultures have interpreted episodes as encounters with otherworldly beings, glimpses of the afterlife, or evidence of a soul separate from the body. These spiritual interpretations, while varying widely, share a common thread: they imbue the experience with profound meaning.

This chapter delves into the intersection of sleep paralysis and spirituality, exploring how the condition has shaped beliefs about the soul, the afterlife, and the boundaries of human consciousness. By examining historical accounts, personal testimonies, and philosophical perspectives, we aim to uncover the deeper truths that lie within these enigmatic episodes.

The Out-of-Body Experience

One of the most compelling and mysterious aspects of sleep paralysis is the sensation of detachment from the physical body, often described as an *out-of-body experience* (OBE). During these episodes, individuals commonly report a profound feeling of disconnection, as though their consciousness has separated from their physical form. This phenomenon can be both unsettling and awe-inspiring, leaving a lasting impression that challenges conventional perceptions of self, reality, and the nature of consciousness.

Many individuals who experience OBEs during sleep paralysis describe a variety of vivid and striking sensations.

For some, the experience begins with an awareness of lightness or weightlessness, as though the physical body has become irrelevant. This is often accompanied by an inexplicable pulling sensation, a vibrational hum, or a feeling of being drawn upward or outward. Those affected frequently report "floating" above their bodies, sometimes observing their physical selves lying motionless below, a perspective that feels remarkably real. Others experience a complete disconnection from their surroundings, transitioning to dreamlike landscapes, tunnels of light, or surreal realms that seem to exist beyond the waking world.

The nature of these out-of-body sensations aligns closely with the state of partial wakefulness and vivid mental imagery that defines sleep paralysis. From a scientific perspective, OBEs are believed to occur due to disruptions in the brain's ability to integrate sensory information about the body's position and orientation in space. The brain typically relies on signals from the vestibular system (which governs balance and spatial awareness) and proprioception (the sense of body position) to maintain an accurate understanding of the self in physical space. During sleep paralysis, when the body is immobilized, but the brain is still partially active, this integration can falter. The result is a disorienting illusion where one's sense of "self" feels displaced or detached, leading to the perception of floating or observing from outside the body.

The vividness of these OBEs is further heightened by the brain's activity during REM (rapid eye movement) sleep. REM sleep is characterized by intense brain activity, particularly in areas associated with memory, imagination, and visual processing. When sleep paralysis occurs at the edge of REM sleep, the mind can produce hyper-realistic visual and sensory experiences that feel indistinguishable from reality. In essence, the brain creates a scenario in which the mind perceives itself as separate from the physical body, even if no actual movement occurs.

However, while science offers neurological explanations, the subjective experience of an out-of-body episode often carries deep emotional and existential significance for those who undergo it. Many individuals describe these moments as profoundly spiritual or transformative. The sensation of detachment from the body, combined with vivid perceptions of alternate planes or dreamlike environments, has led some to interpret OBEs as evidence of the soul or consciousness existing independently of the physical form. This belief resonates with spiritual traditions across cultures, where the idea of a "soul" or "astral body" traveling beyond the physical self is a recurring theme.

For instance, in ancient Egyptian mythology, the *ka* was believed to be the vital essence or double that could leave the body during sleep and traverse the spiritual world. Similarly, Hindu and Buddhist philosophies discuss the "subtle body" or *sukshma sharira*, a spiritual counterpart capable of traveling beyond physical limitations. Shamanic traditions around the world also describe the ability to separate the spirit from the body during trance states to journey to other realms for healing, guidance, or wisdom. Modern accounts of OBEs during sleep paralysis echo these timeless narratives, suggesting that the phenomenon taps into a universal human experience that transcends cultural and temporal boundaries.

The emotional impact of an out-of-body experience during sleep paralysis can vary widely. For some, the sensation is peaceful and even euphoric, providing a sense of freedom and wonder. They describe feelings of lightness, joy, and connection to something greater than themselves. For others, however, the experience can be frightening, especially when combined with the inability to move and unsettling visual or auditory hallucinations. The sudden awareness of being "outside" the body can trigger panic, confusion, or an overwhelming sense of vulnerability.

Interestingly, many individuals who experience OBEs during sleep paralysis find that the episodes become less frightening over time. By learning to remain calm and accept the sensations, some people report gaining a degree of control over the experience. Techniques such as focused breathing, visualization, or intentionally "rolling" out of the body in a mental sense can allow individuals to deepen and explore the out-of-body state. For those who embrace the phenomenon, OBEs become opportunities for exploration and personal insight, transforming an initially unsettling event into something meaningful and even profound.

Modern research into OBEs continues to shed light on this enigmatic phenomenon. Neurologists and psychologists study the brain's mechanisms during these episodes to understand how the mind constructs a sense of self and spatial awareness. Some researchers suggest that OBEs during sleep paralysis may share common ground with near-death experiences (NDEs) or hallucinations induced by altered states of consciousness, such as meditation or sensory deprivation. In all these cases, the brain appears capable of creating powerful and convincing perceptions that challenge the boundaries between reality and imagination.

Ultimately, the out-of-body experience during sleep paralysis remains one of the most fascinating and mysterious aspects of the phenomenon. Whether viewed through the lens of science, spirituality, or personal experience, it invites profound questions about the nature of consciousness, the limits of perception, and the human capacity for transcendence. For those who experience it, the sensation of detachment can serve as a reminder of the extraordinary complexity of the mind and its ability to blur the lines between the physical and the immaterial. While the origins of OBEs may lie in the brain's intricate processes, their impact on the individual—both emotionally and existentially—reveals a deeper truth: that even in moments of stillness, the human spirit possesses the power to explore, reflect, and expand its understanding of itself and the world beyond.

Astral Projection and Sleep Paralysis

The concept of astral projection—the belief that the soul or consciousness can leave the physical body and travel across different realms or dimensions—has origins that stretch back to ancient spiritual and cultural traditions. Rooted in belief systems such as ancient Egyptian mysticism, Hindu Vedanta, and indigenous shamanic practices, astral projection is often described as a deliberate or spontaneous separation of the spiritual self, sometimes called the "astral body," from the physical self. Practitioners and believers describe experiences of exploring distant places, encountering otherworldly entities, or gaining profound spiritual insight during these journeys. While science typically frames astral projection as a phenomenon tied to altered states of consciousness or vivid dream states, its enduring significance across cultures speaks to humanity's desire to transcend the limits of physical existence and explore the mysteries of the unseen.

Sleep paralysis often mirrors what practitioners describe as the initial stages of astral projection. During episodes of sleep paralysis, individuals frequently report sensations that align closely with accounts of astral travel. These include intense vibrations coursing through the body, a feeling of weightlessness or floating, and auditory phenomena such as humming, buzzing, or whooshing sounds. Some individuals also describe a sensation of "tunneling"—a feeling as though they are being pulled through a dark or luminous passage at great speed. These experiences, while disorienting for many, are often interpreted by astral projection practitioners as signs that the soul or consciousness is preparing to leave the body.

The overlap between sleep paralysis and astral projection may be tied to the brain's altered activity during the transition between REM sleep and wakefulness. During sleep paralysis, the brain is partially awake while the body remains immobilized in a state of REM atonia, the natural paralysis that prevents physical movements during dreams. This creates a hybrid state of consciousness in which vivid hallucinations and heightened awareness can occur. The sensation of floating, for instance, may arise from the brain's inability to process spatial orientation while in this liminal state. Similarly, the "vibrational state" often described by individuals may stem from heightened sensory misinterpretations or neural activity within the brainstem.

Despite scientific explanations, many individuals remain convinced of the spiritual nature of these experiences. For practitioners of astral projection, sleep paralysis is seen not as a malfunction but as an opportunity—an entry point into a higher state of awareness. By overcoming fear and remaining calm during sleep paralysis episodes, individuals can, according to astral projection techniques, guide themselves into an out-of-body experience.

Techniques such as focusing on the sensation of lightness, visualizing the separation of the astral body, or mentally "rolling out" of the physical body are often recommended. Practitioners claim that with practice, the experience can be consciously controlled, allowing them to travel to distant locations, explore spiritual realms, or even communicate with beings they perceive as guides or guardians.

Cultural narratives surrounding astral projection further reinforce its connection to sleep paralysis. In ancient Egyptian beliefs, the "ka," or the spiritual double of the body, was said to leave during sleep and travel to the earth or the afterlife. Similarly, in Hindu and Buddhist traditions, the concept of the "subtle body" or "sukshma sharira" describes a spiritual essence capable of traversing realms beyond the material world. Shamanic cultures have long spoken of journeys undertaken during altered states, where the shaman's spirit departs the body to gain wisdom, healing, or insight from other realms. These parallels across cultures highlight a deep-rooted human fascination with the possibility of transcending the body, a theme that sleep paralysis naturally evokes through its vivid and otherworldly sensations.

Modern accounts of astral projection often intertwine with contemporary sleep paralysis experiences. Online forums and personal anecdotes are filled with stories of individuals who, after initial panic during sleep paralysis, learned to embrace the experience and use it as a springboard for astral travel. These individuals frequently describe profound journeys—exploring surreal landscapes, witnessing ethereal light, or feeling a deep sense of unity and peace. While skeptics may dismiss such experiences as highly vivid dreams or neurological phenomena, for those who undergo them, the emotional and spiritual impact is undeniably real.

Ultimately, the relationship between sleep paralysis and astral projection bridges science and spirituality. Sleep paralysis provides a unique, hybrid state of consciousness that mirrors descriptions of out-of-body experiences, offering fertile ground for both scientific inquiry and spiritual exploration. Whether viewed as a neurological anomaly or a gateway to the unseen, these experiences challenge our understanding of the boundaries between body, mind, and consciousness. For many, astral projection—spurred by sleep paralysis—represents not just an escape from fear but an invitation to explore the unknown, transforming an unsettling phenomenon into a profound journey of self-discovery.

Case Study: A Journey Beyond the Body

Jamal, a 34-year-old from Egypt, recounts his journey with sleep paralysis not as a source of fear but as an extraordinary pathway to what he describes as "astral travel." Like many others, Jamal's initial encounters with sleep paralysis were marked by terror and helplessness. The immobilizing sensation, combined with vivid hallucinations of shadowy figures and intense chest pressure, left him questioning both his physical safety and his sanity. However, instead of succumbing to fear, Jamal decided to approach his experiences with curiosity and openness, a shift that transformed his relationship with sleep paralysis entirely.

Jamal began to notice that amidst the immobilization, there was also a peculiar sensation of weightlessness. This feeling, he observed, often coincided with a heightened awareness of his surroundings, as though he were existing on a plane between wakefulness and dreaming. Fascinated by this state, he experimented with his focus during episodes, letting go of the fear and instead channeling his attention to the sensation of lightness. Over time, what had once been an overwhelming sense of entrapment evolved into an opportunity for exploration.

As Jamal deepened his practice, he reported experiencing vivid and surreal journeys that extended beyond the confines of his physical body. He described soaring through vast, otherworldly landscapes filled with luminous colors, unearthly beings, and intricate structures that seemed to defy the laws of physics. These landscapes felt as real to him as the waking world, imbued with a sense of awe and spiritual significance. Jamal interpreted these experiences as visits to spiritual realms, places that offered profound insights and an overwhelming sense of peace.

One particularly vivid episode left a lasting impression on Jamal. He found himself hovering above a shimmering expanse of light that pulsed with energy, resembling an ocean made of pure luminescence. As he "floated" closer, he felt an overwhelming sense of unity and connection, as though he were merging with the very fabric of existence. The experience, as he described, was both humbling and transformative, leaving him with a newfound appreciation for life and the mysteries of consciousness.

Jamal's interpretation of these journeys was deeply shaped by his cultural and spiritual background. Growing up in a region rich with stories of the supernatural and the divine, he viewed his experiences through a spiritual lens. He believed that these episodes allowed him to transcend the physical plane, connecting with realms that are typically inaccessible during ordinary consciousness. For Jamal, sleep paralysis was not merely a neurological glitch but a sacred doorway to deeper truths about the universe and the soul.

Jamal's journey highlights an important aspect of sleep paralysis: its potential to be more than a source of fear and distress. For those like Jamal who choose to explore its boundaries, sleep paralysis can become an opportunity for profound introspection, self-discovery, and even spiritual awakening. His story serves as a reminder that within the unsettling nature of this phenomenon lies the potential for transformative experiences, challenging conventional understandings of what it means to dream, to wake, and to exist.

Scientific Perspectives on the Out-of-Body Experience

While spiritual traditions view out-of-body sensations as evidence of the soul's mobility, neuroscientists attribute them to disruptions in the brain's spatial awareness networks. The temporoparietal junction, a region involved in self-perception, is often implicated in these experiences. Despite these explanations, the profound emotional and spiritual impact of such episodes remains undeniable.

Encounters with Otherworldly Beings

One of the most universally reported aspects of sleep paralysis is the presence of entities. These figures, often described as shadowy, malevolent, or ethereal, have been interpreted as spiritual beings in many cultures.

Angels, Demons, and Spirits

In religious contexts, sleep paralysis entities are frequently seen as angels or demons. For some, these beings represent divine messages or tests of faith; for others, they embody malevolent forces attempting to harm the soul.

Example: Religious Interpretations

- In Christian theology, the paralysis and visions may be seen as encounters with angels or trials sent by God.
- In Hinduism, the sensation of pressure on the chest has been interpreted as the presence of a deity or spirit guiding the soul.

Guardian Spirits or Ancestors

In some cultures, the figures seen during sleep paralysis are believed to be protective spirits or ancestors. These interpretations provide comfort, framing the experience as a spiritual connection rather than an attack.

Cultural Perspective: The Role of Ancestral Spirits

In many African and Afro-Caribbean traditions, sleep paralysis episodes are viewed as moments of ancestral guidance. The immobilization is seen not as a threat but as a means for the ancestors to communicate important messages or warnings.

The Soul and Its Journey

Sleep paralysis raises profound questions about the nature of the soul and its relationship to the body. Many who experience it describe a heightened sense of spiritual awareness, as though touching a deeper reality.

Philosophical Perspectives

The sensation of sleep paralysis aligns with philosophical inquiries into dualism—the idea that the mind and body are distinct entities. René Descartes, for example, proposed that the soul resides in the pineal gland, acting as a bridge between the physical and metaphysical realms. Sleep paralysis, with its sense of disconnection, seems to echo this idea.

Near-Death Experiences

There are striking similarities between sleep paralysis and near-death experiences (NDEs), including sensations of floating, seeing a bright light, or encountering beings of light. These parallels have led some researchers to suggest that sleep paralysis may offer a glimpse into the mechanisms underlying NDEs, further blurring the line between physiology and spirituality.

Mystical Practices and Interpretations

Many spiritual practices seek to induce altered states of consciousness similar to those experienced during sleep paralysis. These practices often frame such states as opportunities for enlightenment or transcendence.

Meditation and Sleep Paralysis

Deep meditation can induce states of physical stillness and mental clarity reminiscent of sleep paralysis. Practitioners of transcendental meditation or Tibetan Dream Yoga often describe sensations of detachment and expanded awareness, viewing them as steps toward spiritual awakening.

Shamanic Journeys

In shamanic traditions, altered states of consciousness are deliberately sought to access spiritual realms. Sleep paralysis episodes, with their vivid hallucinations and sense of otherworldliness, closely resemble the experiences reported by shamans during their journeys.

Transforming Fear into Spiritual Growth

For many, the fear associated with sleep paralysis stems from a lack of understanding. Reframing the experience as a spiritual opportunity rather than a threat can lead to profound personal growth.

Embracing the Unknown

Learning to accept and even welcome sleep paralysis episodes can transform fear into curiosity. Techniques such as mindfulness and visualization can help individuals focus on the sensations without resistance, opening the door to deeper spiritual insights.

Case Study: Overcoming Fear Through Acceptance Amara, a 42-year-old yoga instructor, initially found her sleep paralysis episodes terrifying. However, after learning about their spiritual significance in her culture, she began using meditation and breath control to approach them with calm and curiosity. Over time, Amara reported experiencing profound states of peace and connection during her episodes.

Bridging Science and Spirituality

Sleep paralysis exists at the intersection of science and spirituality, offering insights into both realms. While neuroscience provides explanations for the physiological and psychological mechanisms involved, spiritual perspectives add depth and meaning to the experience.

The Dual Lens Approach

By acknowledging both scientific and spiritual dimensions, individuals can gain a more comprehensive understanding of sleep paralysis. This dual approach not only demystifies the condition but also highlights its potential as a tool for self-discovery.

Reflections on the Infinite

Sleep paralysis invites us to confront profound questions about existence, consciousness, and the nature of reality. Whether interpreted as a neurological anomaly or a spiritual encounter, it holds the power to expand our understanding of ourselves and the world around us.

In the final chapter, we will synthesize the insights gained throughout this journey, offering a holistic perspective on sleep paralysis and its implications for the human experience. For now, we leave readers with the realization that even in moments of stillness, there is movement—toward understanding, growth, and the infinite unknown.

Chapter 16:

Integrating the Mystery—A Holistic Approach to Sleep Paralysis

S leep paralysis is a phenomenon that bridges the boundaries of science, spirituality, art, and psychology. It is not confined to a single explanation or discipline; instead, it invites us to explore deeper questions about reality, consciousness, and human potential. This chapter brings together the various perspectives explored throughout this book, transforming sleep paralysis from a source of fear into an opportunity for profound discovery and personal growth.

From a scientific standpoint, sleep paralysis occurs at the intersection of sleep cycles, most notably during transitions between REM sleep and wakefulness. During these moments, the brain's mechanisms for immobilizing the body during dreams remain active, creating a disconnect between consciousness and physical movement. This natural phenomenon, known as REM atonia, can be startling when experienced while awake. The vivid hallucinations often accompanying these episodes arise from heightened activity in the brain's amygdala, the center for processing fear, and mismatches in how sensory information is integrated. While this physiological understanding demystifies the experience, it also highlights the importance of maintaining healthy sleep habits, such as a consistent sleep schedule and stress management, to reduce the likelihood of episodes.

Yet, science alone cannot fully explain the deeply personal and often surreal experiences of sleep paralysis. The content and perception of these episodes are heavily influenced by individual psychology. Personal fears, cultural narratives, and unresolved emotions shape how the phenomenon manifests. For some, these episodes become a stage for confronting deeply buried anxieties, while for others, they are woven into spiritual or existential beliefs. Understanding these psychological dynamics allows individuals to approach their episodes with awareness and resilience. Practices such as therapy, mindfulness, and self-reflection offer tools for transforming these experiences into pathways of emotional healing and self-discovery.

Sleep paralysis is often interpreted as more than a neurological anomaly. Across cultures and throughout history, it has been seen as a gateway to otherworldly realms. Some view it as a moment of astral projection, where the soul momentarily leaves the body. In contrast, others interpret it as a chance to connect with ancestral spirits or divine entities. These spiritual interpretations challenge conventional ideas of reality, suggesting that sleep paralysis may serve as a bridge between the known and the unknown. For those open to exploring this perspective, reframing sleep paralysis as a spiritual opportunity rather than a threat can shift fear into curiosity. Practices such as meditation, dream journaling, and visualization help individuals integrate these episodes into their broader spiritual journey, fostering a sense of meaning and connection.

Fear is a common reaction to sleep paralysis, but it does not have to dominate the experience. Practical strategies can empower individuals to regain control and transform episodes into manageable events. Grounding techniques, such as focusing on physical sensations like breathing or the feel of the bed, help anchor the mind and body during episodes. Cognitive reframing—recognizing the experience as temporary and natural—reduces its emotional impact. For those interested in lucid dreaming, developing the ability to recognize and navigate dream states can provide confidence and even a sense of mastery over sleep paralysis. Visualization is another powerful tool; imagining protective symbols, such as a shield of light, can shift the emotional tone of an episode, transforming it from a terrifying ordeal into a moment of empowerment.

The surreal nature of sleep paralysis has long inspired artistic and creative expression. Many artists, writers, and musicians have drawn on the vivid and otherworldly imagery of their episodes to create works that resonate deeply with others. Creative outlets such as painting, photography, writing, and composing music provide a way to externalize and process these intense experiences. For instance, one artist's transformation of shadowy figures from her episodes into a hauntingly beautiful photo series not only helped her reclaim her narrative but also offered viewers a glimpse into the complex interplay of fear, beauty, and connection. Such acts of creation turn personal struggles into universal expressions of the human condition.

For those who experience sleep paralysis, connection with others can be transformative. Sharing stories in support groups, online forums, or workshops helps to foster understanding and reduce feelings of isolation. In these spaces, individuals find validation and solidarity, recognizing the shared humanity of their experiences. Beyond personal connections, raising awareness about sleep paralysis through education and storytelling can reduce stigma and promote empathy on a broader scale. As more people understand the condition, those affected may feel less isolated and more empowered to seek resources and support.

Integrating sleep paralysis into daily life involves a balanced approach that combines practical, psychological, and spiritual strategies. Maintaining a healthy lifestyle—including regular sleep schedules, stress management, and physical well-being—is fundamental. Cultivating mindful acceptance of the phenomenon approaching it with curiosity rather than fear, can diminish its emotional impact. For those inclined, the experience can also catalyze creative and spiritual exploration, opening doors to new ways of understanding themselves and their place in the universe. Facing the challenges of sleep paralysis fosters resilience, teaching individuals to confront fears, embrace the unknown, and emerge stronger and more self-aware.

Despite advancements in science and psychology, sleep paralysis retains an aura of mystery. It invites profound questions about the nature of consciousness, the boundaries of reality, and the interplay between mind, body, and spirit. These questions remind us of the vast unknowns that remain within ourselves and the universe, urging us to continue exploring with curiosity and wonder.

Sleep paralysis, though unsettling, offers profound opportunities for growth, connection, and discovery. It challenges individuals to expand their understanding of human potential and confront their fears with courage. As readers close this chapter, they carry with them practical tools, insights, and a renewed sense of curiosity. Sleep paralysis serves as a powerful reminder that even in moments of stillness, there is potential for movement—toward healing, transformation, and a deeper understanding of the mysteries that shape our lives.

Sleep paralysis is a condition that, while unsettling, offers profound opportunities for growth, exploration, and connection. Whether viewed through the lens of science, spirituality, or creativity, it challenges us to confront our fears and expand our understanding of human potential.

Chapter 17:

Bridging Science, Spirituality, and the Human Experience: The Mystery of Sleep Paralysis The final chapter

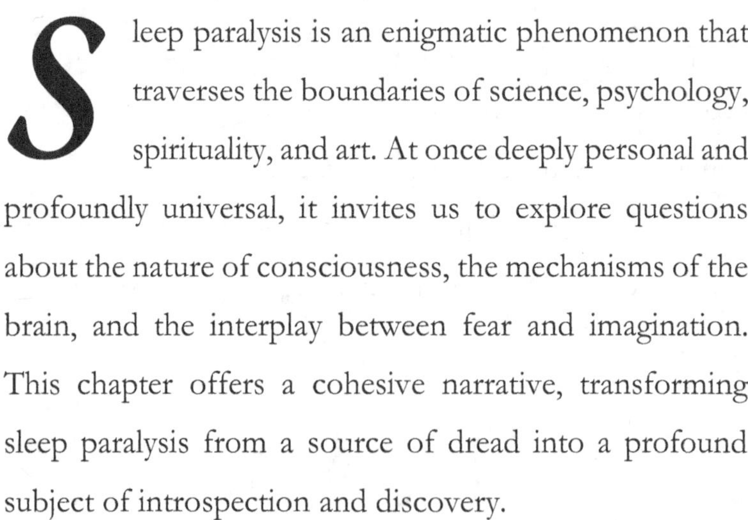

Sleep paralysis is an enigmatic phenomenon that traverses the boundaries of science, psychology, spirituality, and art. At once deeply personal and profoundly universal, it invites us to explore questions about the nature of consciousness, the mechanisms of the brain, and the interplay between fear and imagination. This chapter offers a cohesive narrative, transforming sleep paralysis from a source of dread into a profound subject of introspection and discovery.

At its essence, sleep paralysis emerges at the fragile intersection of sleep and wakefulness. This delicate transition often occurs during REM sleep, a phase characterized by vivid dreams and a state of muscular atonia designed to prevent physical movements. This atonia, regulated by brainstem structures like the locus coeruleus, can occasionally malfunction, leaving an individual conscious but physically immobilized.

During such moments, the brain's fear and arousal circuits—particularly the amygdala—are hyperactive, intensifying feelings of dread and facilitating vivid, often terrifying hallucinations. These episodes are a testament to the intricate and sometimes imperfect workings of our neurological systems, where slight disruptions in neurotransmitter release can result in extraordinary experiences.

The brain's neurochemistry plays an essential role in these events. Neurotransmitters like dopamine and serotonin, which govern mood, alertness, and sleep transitions, can influence the frequency and intensity of sleep paralysis episodes. Stress disrupts sleep patterns, and underlying mental health conditions often exacerbate imbalances in these chemicals, increasing the likelihood of an episode. Scientific studies provide a fascinating window into this biochemical interplay, shedding light on how emotions, physiology, and perception intertwine during moments of sleep paralysis.

But beyond its scientific explanations, sleep paralysis resonates with the deep human desire to assign meaning to extraordinary experiences. Across cultures and throughout history, it has been interpreted through spiritual and supernatural lenses. Ancient civilizations saw it as a form of divine encounter—moments where the boundaries between the earthly and the ethereal dissolved. Even today, some describe episodes as opportunities for astral projection or spiritual connection, viewing the phenomenon as a gateway to realms beyond our waking reality. Such perspectives, while challenging scientific norms, underscore the richness of human imagination and belief systems.

Cultural narratives and personal psychology further shape how individuals interpret their experiences of sleep paralysis. The shadowy figures, pressure on the chest, and distorted sounds commonly reported during episodes are not just physiological artifacts; they reflect individual fears, cultural archetypes, and unresolved emotions. This blending of biology and belief is what makes sleep paralysis so compelling. For some, these episodes are traumatic, evoking primal fears of vulnerability and isolation. For others, they become opportunities to confront deep-seated anxieties or explore their inner worlds.

Art and creativity offer a powerful way to process and transcend the unsettling nature of sleep paralysis. Writers, artists, and musicians have drawn inspiration from their experiences, transforming the surreal and often frightening imagery of their episodes into works of profound beauty and meaning.

The act of Creating provides a means to externalize fear, reclaim agency, and connect with others who share similar experiences. Through art, sleep paralysis becomes not just a personal struggle but a universal narrative about the human condition, exploring themes of vulnerability, resilience, and transformation.

The mental health dimension of sleep paralysis adds yet another layer to its complexity. Conditions like anxiety, depression, and bipolar disorder are often linked to an increased prevalence of episodes. The heightened arousal states associated with anxiety, the disrupted sleep patterns in depression, and the erratic energy cycles in bipolar disorder all create fertile ground for the neurological misfires that characterize sleep paralysis. Recognizing these connections allows for targeted interventions, such as therapy, stress reduction, and sleep hygiene practices, helping individuals regain control and reduce the frequency of episodes.

Personal stories bring the phenomenon to life, illustrating its diverse manifestations and the ways individuals navigate its challenges. For Jacob, a teacher plagued by recurrent sleep paralysis, understanding the neurological basis of his condition was empowering. His journey— marked by improved sleep habits and a deeper understanding of his brain's workings—transformed a source of fear into an opportunity for self-growth. Similarly, countless individuals have shared how reframing sleep paralysis as a gateway to lucid dreaming has opened doors to profound creative and psychological insights, allowing them to navigate the dream world with newfound awareness and purpose.

Ultimately, sleep paralysis is a condition that reflects the duality of human experience: it is at once a source of vulnerability and a wellspring of potential. It challenges us to confront our fears, expand our understanding of consciousness, and find meaning in experiences that defy easy explanations. The scientific mechanisms underlying sleep paralysis may be rooted in the brain's intricate sleep-wake systems. Still, its impact extends far beyond biology, touching on spirituality, art, and the profound depths of human psychology.

As we conclude this exploration, it is clear that sleep paralysis is more than an unsettling anomaly. It is a gateway to discovery, inviting us to question the nature of reality, embrace the mysteries of the mind, and confront the fears that lie within. Whether viewed through the lens of science, creativity, or spirituality, it offers a unique opportunity to deepen our understanding of ourselves and the interconnectedness of mind and body.

In moments of paralysis, when the body is still, but the mind is awake, there lies the potential for profound insight and transformation. Sleep paralysis reminds us that even in moments of fear and vulnerability, there is beauty and resilience—a testament to the extraordinary within the ordinary. It invites us to approach the unknown with curiosity and wonder, uncovering the hidden depths of our consciousness and the infinite possibilities of human experience.

www.ingramcontent.com/pod-product-compliance
Lightning Source LLC
Chambersburg PA
CBHW061624250726
48659CB00004B/1073